build a

better

Book

Club

By the Same Authors

HARRY HEFT

On Your Mark: Getting Better Marks at University Without Working Harder or Being Smarter, with David Kinahan (Macmillan Canada). Published in the u.s. as *The Savvy Student* (Avon Books).

PETER O'BRIEN

Introduction to Literature: British, American, Canadian, co-edited with Robert Lecker and Jack David (Harper & Row)
So to Speak: Interviews with Contemporary Canadian Writers, editor (Vehicule)
Fatal Recurrences: New Fiction in English from Montreal, co-edited with Hugh Hood (Vehicule)

build a better
better
Book
Club

Harry Heft

and

Peter O'Brien

Macmillan Canada

Canadian Cataloguing in Publication Data

Heft, Harold, 1964–
  Build a better book club

ISBN 0-7715-7621-8

1. Book clubs. I. O'Brien, Peter, 1957–   . II. Title.

LC6619.H43 1999   028'.8   C99-930051-2

This book is available at special discounts for bulk purchases by your group or organization for sales promotions, premiums, fundraising and seminars. For details, contact: Macmillan Canada, Special Sales Department, 29 Birch Avenue, Toronto, ON M4V 1E2. Tel: 416-963-8830.

Cover and interior design: Counterpunch/Peter Ross
Cover illustration: Michela Sorrentino Design
Back-cover photograph: Suzanne Mitchell and Trish Tervit
Typesetting: Linda Mackey

Macmillan Canada
CDG Books Canada Inc.
Toronto, Ontario, Canada

We acknowledge the financial support of the Government of Canada through the Book Publishing Industry Development Program for our publishing activities.

1 2 3 4 5   TRANS-B-G   03 02 01 00 99

Printed in Canada

This book is dedicated to Suzanne, with love,
and to Lorne "Pudge" Aaron, with friendship;

and, with love, to Sheilagh,
and to Siobhan, who will enjoy writing in it
and ripping out its pages.

Acknowledgements and Thanks

Some of the quotations from friends and fellow book club members that have been used in this book are amalgamations or adaptations. It's not quite right to say that "all characters in this book are fictitious and any resemblance to actual persons, living or dead, is purely coincidental," but we have freely crafted some of the stories and insights that people shared with us. We did this to protect the identity of some who choose to remain anonymous and to assist our own efforts in capturing germane, relevant commentary.

We would like to graciously thank the following people, who either read and commented on earlier drafts of this book, or provided creative, intellectual or culinary inspiration of one sort or another: Lorène Bourgeois, Susan Cunningham, Karina Dahlin, Penny Daniêls, Eddie and Ruby Heft, Joel Heft, Richard Heft, Sara Kamal, Cynthia Langille, Peter Legris, Avon MacFarlane, Martha McLeod, Gail Misra, Suzanne Mitchell, Al Nausedas, Bridget O'Brien, Bernadette and John O'Connell, Sheilagh O'Connell, Joan Randall, Mark Rowlinson, Bob Shantz, Christopher Shantz, Alison Smiley, Sarah Smiley, Mary Stinson, Julie Stone, Barbara Track and Cathy Yanosik.

And thanks to members of our book group, whose ideas, personalities, observations and general enthusiasm about reading we have freely stolen in the interest of fuelling this book. These inspirational book club members are the aforementioned Al and Suzanne, as well as Jennifer Mason, Wes Moon, Marden Paul, Joel Porter, David Vella, Vicki Vokas, Brenda Wilson, Mary Wilson, Tara Wilson and Jennifer Wood. We also thank the Madison Pub in Toronto for welcoming our book club month after month, and for keeping the calamari warm and the beer cold.

We would also like to thank our agent, David Johnston, at Livingston Cooke and our editor, Jill Lambert, at Macmillan for their encouragement, guidance and good humour.

Contents

Foreword

by Paul Quarrington, author

My friend Alan (the author has introduced this character kind of abruptly—do you think this is a good idea?) loves to debate, to posit and argufy. (Do you think the author really meant to use the word "argufy"?) Often, when things get heated, Alan will lift his forefingers into the air and describe a rectangle, approximately eight inches by five. "We're in the Box," he'll announce, by which he means, one is no longer allowed to get angry. Ideas no longer have the power to wound; they must now be regarded dispassionately. It may sound merely like a cowardly way for Alan to avoid a bloody nose, but the Box is, once you're used to it, a truly invigorating place to be.

I've decided that it's no coincidence that Alan's imaginary Box is about the same size and shape as a book. A book is a place where one can romp and play with ideas and not get hurt. So, if a book is a kind of playground (the author has introduced, and is now belaboring, an analogy), then who would want to enter alone? "The more the merrier" was my philosophy when I was five years old, and I have been given little reason to change.

That's why I think book clubs are such a grand idea. I encourage you all to form and/or join one. This book will tell you all you need to know about doing so.

I was invited by Harry and Peter, the nice fellows who wrote this book, to attend a meeting of their book club, wherein the members discussed my novel *Whale Music*. I went along willingly, even eagerly. Now it is true that this meeting was held in a bar, and it usually requires little inducement to lure me inside such establishments. But mostly I wanted to romp and play with ideas, even if they were mine, or at least had originated with me.

Here's why: Let us say that a book is like a voyage down a big river. (The author has abandoned his "playground" analogy and is now hastily suggesting another—is that fair?) No passenger has a complete sense of the journey—those with starboard berths see different things than those on the port. My point is, even the captain doesn't know the whole of the trip, concentrating as he is on avoiding the treacherous riverbanks. Well, perhaps you could use the preceding as a warm-up, a kind of test-drive, for your book club meeting. What exactly am I talking about?

I remember studying some story in school. The teacher was going on about the inherent symbolism, and the entire class rose up as one and declaimed that surely the writer could not have been thinking about such things as he wrote the story. Well, all these years later, I've decided that the class was right. The writer doesn't think about such things—any writer who is reflecting actively on the symbolism is composing a story that I probably don't want to read. But it is definitely coming out of the writer, who is creating with the whole of his or her being. The writer is, you see, like the ship's captain, focused on avoiding disaster. It is therefore of great interest for the writer to learn that, at one point, a whale drifted by, spouting root beer out its blowhole.

(The author has gone too far.)

So form or join a book club, and invite an author to visit. (Hey—invite me to visit! My new book, *The Spirit Cabinet*, is about magic, and I've learned some ginchy tricks.)

Read books: that is, climb into the Box, romp and play with ideas.

Because—I may not have mentioned—it's fun.

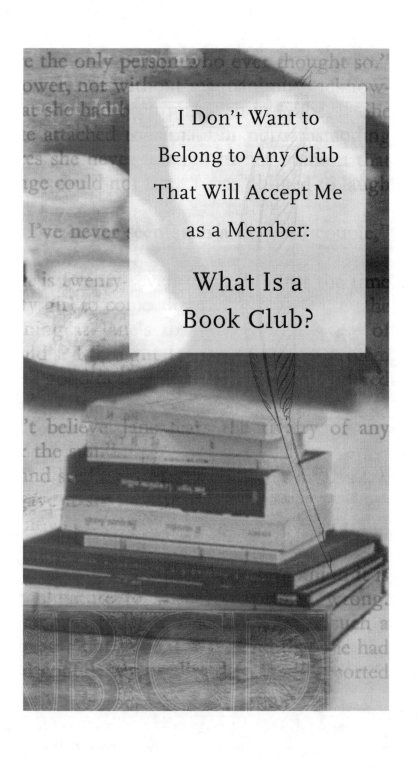

I Don't Want to
Belong to Any Club
That Will Accept Me
as a Member:

What Is a
Book Club?

> *When village-maids in scatter'd groups are seen,*
> *And rustics urge the foot-ball o'er the green;*
> *Within the bosom of this fam'd retreat,*
> *The motley members of the Book-club meet.*
>
> CHARLES SHILLITO,
> "THE COUNTRY BOOK-CLUB: A POEM," 1790

Start Me Up

A book club is really nothing more than a group of people, perhaps like-minded but not necessarily so, who enjoy reading or would like to add a more structured and perhaps more satisfying way of reading to their lives. The members gather together periodically to discuss books and the adventures that await them within the many pages of fiction and non-fiction.

The book club—or reading group, or book discussion group, or salon (it goes by many names)—might start with one person or a couple of friends from the same office or shop floor or neighbourhood. They notice one of their friends or colleagues reading a book or a magazine article that intrigues them or that they have already read and enjoyed. They begin to discuss the book or article and recognize the potential for a more structured meeting to take place. After ferreting out other potential members, a few more are gathered and this loose association of active readers meets in a basement or at a pub or around a kitchen table.

Or the club may come out of a group of close friends who have shared other experiences together (travel, school, kids, hobbies) and then decided that a creative or intellectual component is missing from their lives. In this situation there is no shock of the new, for the members of the group are already comfortable with one another, but shifting gears and providing the structure of a reading group will still create some ups and downs.

Taking that first step in forming a book club is sometimes the most daunting part of the process. *Build a Better Book Club* will help you get over the "opening night" jitters. It will help you get your book club on solid ground, ready to soar. It will help you establish a book club that is built to last and that will be both challenging and fun. After all, "reading is to the mind what exercise is to the body," as the great essayist and editor Richard Steele said. As we all know, sometimes we need a little prodding to get ourselves into the gym for the first time, or on an exercise regime that lasts more than just a few days.

For those of you who are currently in a book club but find that it is beginning to lose its focus or excitement, or is being torn apart by disruptive or bored members, this book will help you get it back on track. It will help you liven up your faltering book club and give you practical tips on how to keep the creative, intellectual and organizational juices flowing. Let's face it, most book clubs wander off after the first blushes of excitement for any number of good reasons. Sometimes it seems easier just to let the whole endeavour fizzle out once the initial burst of enthusiasm fades a little. But there are simple and effective ways to spruce up your discussion group and this book will show you how.

The Pleasure Principle

The pleasures gathered within the pages of fiction and non-fiction books are, of course, many and various. Anyone who reads knows that remarkable ability that books have to take us out of ourselves, to allow us to travel to lands real or imagined that we may never be able to visit any other way. "There is no frigate like a book," said Emily Dickinson. Like all readers, she knew the power that books have to set a mirror up to our real lives as well as our imaginary lives, to provide a new perspective on the creative, intellectual and psychological landscapes we inhabit.

As children we all learn the joys of reading, being read to and then sharing our opinions and observations with others, even if it's only "Why is that bear named Pooh?" or "Do bears really eat honey?" For many of us, one of the joys of our childhood was being read to by our parents or other family members parts of the Bible or the Madeline books, or Charles Dickens' *A Christmas Carol*, or J. R. R. Tolkien's *The Lord of the Rings* or any number of others. We are, both as children and adults, curious and inquisitive by nature. One of the reasons we continue to read throughout our lives is to sustain this innate sense of wonder and excitement. Reading is truly one of life's most challenging and joyful activities, a pastime that can be enjoyed when we are three as much as when we are ninety. And unlike some other activities that please and satiate us, our appetite and desire for books seems to get stronger throughout our lives. As Lucy, one of our fellow book club members, says: "reading is all about pleasure... pushing your boundaries and those of others, talking with people who also feel passionately about books, learning to see the world the way other people do. These are, for me, exciting and satisfying things to do."

Build a Better Book Club will encourage you to recapture the wonder and excitement you had when you first learned to read. Book clubs are one way to keep those initial enthusiasms and sympathies you had as a child well stoked throughout your life. By gathering together with others whom you may know intimately or perhaps not so intimately, you can share threads of your imagination and fantasies, your questions and your fears, all the while pushing your own intellectual and creative boundaries. Who knows, you may even find a few life-long partners in the process. Good friends and more than a few romances have resulted from the close and forgiving confines of a book club. At the very least, you'll have fun, add a sparkle to your mind and sharpen your opinions about books and the people with whom you read them.

For those interested in the liveliness and good-natured tension of interpersonal connections, the book club that meets regularly over food and drink is a very rewarding and fulfilling encounter. We have friends who consider their book clubs as "a lifeline into the world of the imagination," or "a way to get away from, even if it's only for a few hours, the rat race of work and kids and mortgage payments and cutting the grass" or, simply, "a load of fun and inspiration."

For those of you who have never been a member of a book club, the group may have a hint of the exclusive private club about it, because membership is sometimes by invitation only. But book clubs can also be a fluid organization of different kinds of people. Some book clubs remain unchanged over many years. The members would never miss a meeting and they often become an important part of people's social and intellectual engagement with other like-minded people. Other book clubs have a much more adaptable nature. They allow new members to join whenever they choose, and the flavour is much more social than intellectual. The form of the book club is strong enough and adaptable enough to accommodate various shapes and configurations.

History Has Many Cunning Passages: A Brief Chronicle of the Book Club

Although they might not have always been referred to as such, book clubs and discussion groups have been with us since before the first books were even produced. The students, disciples and hangers-on who gathered around philosophers Plato and Aristotle did so to listen and perhaps to add their own faltering or inspired observations about what the great men were thinking and speaking of at the time. In Raphael's great painting *The School of Athens*, Plato and Aristotle debate in the centre of the canvas, perhaps about the joys and struggles of democratic life, while all around them people talk, gesticulate or seem lost in thought.

In medieval times storytellers travelled from town to town to share their renditions of well-known verse poems that were full of wisdom and entertainment. Poems such as *Beowulf* and *The Wanderer* have perhaps been recited many more times than they have ever been reprinted in books. "Attend!"—the first word of *Beowulf*—is there for a reason. It's as though the speaker claps to attract the attention of the listeners gathered to hear the recitation of the poem.

For centuries, people have gathered in coffee houses, restaurants and bars to read and discuss the literature of the day, or to debate the political tract of the moment. They shared their observations with others of the new instalment of a George Eliot story or a recent magazine article. *The Tatler* and *The Spectator*, magazines edited by Richard Steele and Joseph Addison, spurred lively and engaged discussions in the eighteenth century on topics as variable as marriage, contemporary fiction and society at large. The aim of *The Spectator* was "to enliven morality with wit, and to temper wit with morality." In the same way today, intriguing, sophisticated or controversial articles in *The New Yorker*, *Harper's*, *Saturday Night* or the local newspaper often spark vigorous discussions and passionate debate among us.

In North America reading discussion groups really took off with the establishment of the Great Books Foundation, founded in 1947 by a group of businessmen in Chicago and led by Robert Maynard Hutchins, president of the University of Chicago. The foundation defines itself as "an independent, nonprofit educational organization whose mission is to provide people of all ages with the opportunity to read, discuss, and learn from outstanding works of literature." Over one million students participate in its Junior Great Books Program, which began in 1962. The foundation also trains more than 15,000 people every year to lead book discussion groups. Despite these huge numbers, there is no question that the foundation still has much work to do: it is estimated that there are approximately 30 million functionally illiterate people in North America today.

It is impossible to know how many book clubs exist in North America today, but it is safe to say that if you join or start a book club, you will not be alone. In cities and towns across the continent, people are gathering together in congenial surroundings, enjoying lively discussions. We are not certain exactly why this idea has suddenly caught fire over the past ten to fifteen years. Perhaps it's part of the cocooning instinct we all have, or perhaps it's a way to build a bulwark against the pervasive and sometimes mind-numbing influence of all the canned laughter and canned emotions of television. The Canada Council program that sends writers across the country to give readings, such series as the Harbourfront Reading Series in Toronto, and shows such as CBC

Radio's "Writers and Company," CBC-TV's "Mid-Day" and TVOntario's "Imprint" also certainly do their part to create interest in books. Whatever the reasons and the causes, the idea of starting a book club has gained momentum over the past decade.

Oprah Winfrey has probably done more to popularize reading than anyone since Guttenberg or Dickens. On her television show, she has also rightly championed many groups of writers previously marginalized, such as women and black writers. Books that gain the much-coveted Oprah stamp of approval become instant best sellers. (We are awaiting the call from her producers telling us that *Build a Better Book Club* has been chosen as an "Oprah Selection.") Even if only a small percentage of her audience goes out and actually buys the recommended book, that still translates into hundreds of thousands of copies sold, which is one reason why you don't meet nearly as many depressed writers these days as you used to. Public libraries have even been calling the Oprah show to find out in advance about her selections so they can begin stacking the shelves in anticipation. Many book clubs have been formed across North America to discuss her inspired choices, often meeting at local bookstores.

The Internet has recently become an important resource for anyone interested in book clubs. It can be used to track down books, order them at discounted prices, generate useful book lists for club members to choose from, and spur ideas that lead to fruitful discussions. It is also the electronic home to many virtual reading clubs, where members may never actually meet the people with whom they talk about books.

Log on to the Internet and type the words "reading group" or "book discussion group" into one of the search engines. You will be surprised at the vast number of resources open to you. Try typing in the title of the book that you are reading, and you can often find a site where numerous people have already offered their insights into that book, and where your observations are equally welcome. Try returning to the site the next day and read the other readers' responses to your comments (make an electronic "book-mark" of the page so you can easily find the site again). If this is your first exposure to book discussions, then you might find such an exchange fascinating, though the effort and time involved may eventually become frustrating to those readers who crave more instant gratification.

One such group that we researched describes itself as "a chatty group who love to read and share our reading experiences with others." Another mentions that its members are gathered from "five different countries [and] read a piece of world litera-ture every two weeks and send their reviews on to each other via e-mail." At another site you can click on a key word so "hundreds of other on-line forums for book lovers become accessible."

The virtual clubs that Oprah and the Internet offer are, in a sense, no-fuss, no-muss. You may not feel comfortable sharing your intimate or innermost thoughts with others whom you hardly know. On the other hand you may choose to share your deepest thoughts and fears precisely because you will never meet these people face to face. The distance created by the television or a computer can, in a curious and liberating way, be very com-forting. Just be careful to avoid so much keyboarding that you develop tendinitis before you finish discussing your first book!

As much as we enjoy and appreciate the types of book discus-sions that take place on the Internet and in other, less personal venues, the type of club that we envision as our model for this book has eight to twelve regular members. They meet on a rela-tively precise schedule (say one to two times per month) and enjoy at least some common interests that guide them in choos-ing books and forming discussions.

Whatever your level of comfort and interest is, there is a book club waiting for you to join or to start yourself. It is a community that is limitless in both size and opportunity. In preparation for this book we interviewed many people from many different back-grounds who belong to numerous varieties of book clubs.

Perhaps it's just the crowds we hang around with, but not one person we talked to did not already belong to a book club or did not have a good friend who was a book club member. Perhaps it is also just the nature of the beast, but all the book club members that we talked to were happy to share their thoughts with us.

In all these permutations of the book club, from the earliest days' to today's, expanding the imagination and the intellect is accompanied by thoughts of friendship, romance, food, drink and lively discussions on a host of issues unrelated to the book or article in question. Of course, the book club is not only an opportunity to read and discuss books: it also provides the opportunity to sharpen your social skills, to dispel any nervousness you may have when speaking in public, to seek out friends for other activities that you enjoy, to push the boundaries of your education or interests, and to discover new ways of seeing the worlds of literature or science. To rephrase that old chestnut: eat, drink, read and be merry, for tomorrow there will be another book to discuss.

I Do: The Importance of Commitment

Some degree of commitment on the part of the members is necessary to form any book club, and it is important at the beginning of things to make this clear. The club need not be set up along military lines or depend on the fervour of religious devotion, but it does have to encourage, and it will ultimately reward, a sense of obligation and responsibility. Our friend Laura says that the best thing about her book club is that "it forces me to read the book and prepare for the upcoming discussion, something that I take very seriously." When we asked her what is the worst thing about the book clubs she has belonged to, she repeated exactly the same phrase. This is not an unusual situation.

Many of us are burdened by a whole range of other responsibilities and obligations. You may be attracted to a book club because it forces you to keep up with reading, and at the same time feel a certain dread when it is just before bed time and you have finally dispatched your various daily obligations: "Yikes, the book club is meeting the day after tomorrow and I still have 200 pages to read! How will I ever find the time to finish the book?" It can be similar to the same sort of dread that came over us when we had an essay due or when we realize that we really can't delay painting the front hallway any longer because the family is arriving next week for a visit.

The challenge is somehow to harness this anxiety and not let it consume the many joys of being in the book club. Later in this book we will talk about the different kinds of people who join book clubs. For now, let's just take this sense of commitment in small steps. One of the best ways we have found to prepare for the meeting is to set out a certain schedule every day or few days for the reading required for your book club. You can read and absorb a lot of reading in only fifteen minutes a day or an hour every third evening.

Another option is to set out a large swath of time, say every Sunday afternoon. The main thing is to provide yourself some structure and stick to it, or you'll soon watch whatever "free" time you do have swallowed up by more mundane and less satisfying activities. Finding the time to read can be a bit like finding the time to exercise—the more you do, the more you find that you have the time to do it. It's all a question of priorities.

If you do find yourself overwhelmed by other commitments, there is no shame in backing out of your group. We have a friend who has joined and left a variety of clubs over the years, depending on her other responsibilities. "Sometimes other things just get in the way," she says "and I feel I can't give the club my all." Although she hasn't remained in any one club for decades, like some of our other friends, she has made a valuable contribution to each club that she has joined.

Another friend has been a member of a theological book club for almost thirty years. As a minister, he uses the book club as a way to test out new ways of thinking that he may not be able to from the pulpit or with his parishioners. He has also read books that he may never had read had it not been for his club. For him the book club that he joined many years ago is one of the defining features of his life: "It really is an important part of my life...so many things I've thought about over the years have resulted from the conversations and discussions that have burst into life in my book club," he says.

Yet another friend, Jeanette, has been in the same book club since 1949. The club formed just after most of its members graduated from university and "we've seen each other through various ups and downs, including the odd divorce." This particular group has defined itself differently over the years. For a few years, members were expected to produce essays on significant works; more recently it has become a form of intellectual friendship among the members.

Define commitment however you would like, but you've got to wrestle with it and you've got to let it win if you want a satisfying club.

One Fish, Two Fish, Red Fish, Blue Fish: The Different Kinds of Clubs

It sometimes seems that our minds work best when they flit randomly from one notion to another. Or perhaps it is more accurate to say that for most of us, our mind's natural default setting seems to be speedy and formless meandering from one topic or fragment to another. Each member of your book club has a multitude of experiences and fears and joys that you may never have experienced yourself. Book clubs are a way to harness the richness of these experiences and, when appropriate, share them with others. We're not talking about book clubs as therapy here, although by definition they are a form of creative and experiential therapy. They do function best, however, when there is a certain random energy present, when a dynamic forms that spurs and inspires all members. At their best, book clubs gather together these disparate experiences or affections and make something new and interesting out of them.

People also, of course, often learn more from their fears and troubles than they do from their joys and happiness. Some of the books that we recommend for getting started may disturb you or bring up real fears. *Night*, by Elie Wiesel, is a harrowing discussion about the Holocaust and the guilt felt by a survivor of the death camps. It is a deeply troubling and disturbing book that may not be to everyone's liking. That it is a masterful story by someone who went on to win a Nobel Peace Prize may not be enough to make everyone in your group comfortable with reading it, but one of the most rewarding things about book clubs is that they encourage you to read material that you may never have sought out on your own.

Most of us have the innate desire to share our thoughts and observations with others. At times we may howl in disapproval or disagreement. We may relish a feisty argument that forces us to think in new ways. And we may enjoy discovering a sympathetic ear or a willing audience for our opinions.

Book clubs take these random acts and provide a certain adaptable structure. People may not be any busier in our age than they have been in other ages, but it does seem we are under more stress. There are, perhaps, more varieties of pressures on our time than at any other time in history. There is also a wide variety of forms of knowledge and entertainment out there to eat up our time. At their best, book clubs create a respite from these multitudinous pressures.

As we mentioned earlier, there are various kinds of book clubs, and one of your most important first steps is deciding which sort best suits your needs. The most common types of clubs are the scholarly or intellectual group, the social club masquerading as a book club, the virtual group and the book friendship group.

The Scholarly or Intellectual Book Club. Most groups usually begin with at least the pretense of defining themselves as being in some way scholarly or intellectual, regardless of the direction they eventually take. This type of club is primarily serious in nature and is founded by people interested in truly stretching their intellect. Often the preparation for these groups is rigorous and the meetings are intense. Members may even generate lists of challenging discussion topics and circulate them in advance of each meeting. Sometimes the discussion of fundamental ideas (socialism versus capitalism; a scientific view of the world versus a theological one) can become argumentative or combative. Specialists in the field trade arcane snippets of historical or biographical minutiae and most members outside these small confines will feel out of place.

Those who join these groups without the necessary degree of commitment or intellectual confidence may invite some resentment from the more dedicated members, or vice versa. When you seek to join a club, or if you are invited to join, always ask in advance about the level and intensity of the group's average discussions. If they do not suit your own level, then it may be best to keep looking.

The Social Club. Often the members who join or start these clubs are more interested in the social aspects, the "meeting friends" part of the proceedings, rather than actually reading the books. They like to say they belong to a book club but it is perhaps more for reasons of cachet than the stimulation that comes from closely reading a well-written and challenging book. For those who truly want to discuss the books at hand, these types of clubs can be very frustrating. For those wanting only some minimal intellectual form to an otherwise purely social event, these can be fun but not particularly challenging.

The Virtual Group. This group, as discussed earlier, is not so much a personal group as it is a disparate and loose association of individuals who may never actually meet. The social interaction is, by definition, at a minimum, but members of such clubs still fully enjoy the challenges and excitement of reading and discussing books with others. We have some friends who belong to regular face-to-face groups and also occasionally participate in virtual groups, when it suits their commitments and interests. The food and the social interaction may not be quite as good if you join an Internet club but if you can't find the structured time to meet regularly, it might be just what you're looking for. Unlike other clubs, the Internet discussion group allows you to read what others think, put in your own two cents' worth, and then turn it all off when it suits your purposes. Real live people are not as easily shut off as a computer, however much they may deserve it sometimes.

The Book Friendship Group. This is perhaps the most common form of group and the type that we will refer to most in these pages. Many book friendship groups have both an intellectual and a social dimension, but they can also define themselves more broadly, integrating activities other than book discussion, such as attending other social or cultural events. This type of club is based on mutual interests related to books and ideas, and it depends on a small gathering of committed friends, neighbours, acquaintances or colleagues. These groups can have profound and long-lasting influence on their members. At best, they are spirited, passionate and lively.

Within these broad categories there are, of course, many sub-sets: the females-only group, the co-ed group, the male group, the group concentrated on only one topic or writer (Jane Austen only, for example, or nothing but mystery novels), the group formed along age or education lines, groups that invite local experts to lead a discussion versus member-led groups, groups led by one person versus those with rotating responsibilities, to name a few other possibilities.

The group you start or are currently a member of may have elements of all or most of the above. One member might have a particular interest in a specific author or genre, a few others may enjoy the camaraderie more than the reading, a few might be good friends outside the group, while others might best be served by a group on the Internet. The challenge is to harness these various strengths and interests into a coherent whole, and that is the responsibility of all members of the group.

The tone of your group may also vary widely, from very formal, with each member speaking for a designated amount of time, to very informal, with all members joining in a free-for-all discussion. Later we will discuss such issues as the intricacies of reading a book closely and critically, and a variety of social issues such as where to meet, and whether or not to have food or drink during the meeting.

For now let us simply note the differences between the member-led group and the expert-led group.

The Member-Led Group is, as it sounds, when some member of the group, or every member sequentially, leads the discussion for that day or that book. The advantages are plentiful: people challenge themselves to think in new ways and to move the discussion forward for all the other members. It can be a powerful and sometimes not-altogether easy thing to lead the discussion of strong and varying personalities.

Our friend Richard's book club ensures that every member gets a crack at leading the group: "not everyone is as comfortable leading the discussion but it's also surprising to see the insights that have come out of people when you least expect it." Another friend says that her group has discovered many interesting elements of peoples' lives: "a Jewish member of our group led us through, in a very informed and impassioned way, a couple of novels by Saul Bellow, while another member spoke quite eloquently about Virginia Woolf, part of which came out of her close reading of Woolf as an undergraduate student. We very quickly learned that everyone has something to teach and, more importantly, everyone has something to learn."

Another advantage of the member-led group is that all members appreciate the trials the leader of the day is going through (assuming, of course, that the duties of leadership rotate among the members), and therefore they are more likely to help sustain the conversation at an engaging or provocative level. To be sure, not every one of your meetings will be full of rapier wit and stunning insights, but they will certainly improve as you go.

The Expert-Led Group enlists the particular talents of a scholar, teacher or other professional. The form is usually a lecture, followed by the discussion, in which the leader may or may not participate. These experts are available almost anywhere. While we were teaching at universities, we had colleagues who hired themselves out for a reasonable price (perhaps $50 or $100 for an hour-long lecture and subsequent discussion) to local book clubs to lecture on numerous topics related to their field of expertise. If your group would enjoy inviting a lecturer under these conditions, call the English department of your local college, university or continuing education program and ask the secretary to recommend someone who may be interested in participating in this type of discussion and who would be entertaining (you will be surprised at how candid most English department secretaries will be under these circumstances). Then just call around—most professors will not balk at the possibility of padding their income.

In many towns and cities you can also find expert lecturers who have started their own book-reading series (at bookstores, libraries or local social centres), where they generate a reading list and then people can subscribe to attend their lectures. These can be very convenient, if you are looking to avoid the commitment or hassle of creating your own book club, or if you favour this type of discussion structure.

The advantages of this form is that members are treated to a person of usually original and well-informed insights who can open up new doors of knowledge better than the average reader ever could. The formality may turn off some members but the level of new information should more than compensate for that. At their best, expert-led meetings inspire all members to ratchet up their preparation for the meeting in question and all subsequent meetings.

Our friend Mark was in a book club that enlisted a local university lecturer to lead the discussion of *The Handmaid's Tale* by Margaret Atwood: "We were really pleased with the presentation: it was witty, and extremely well-informed. The professor brought in all sorts of biographical information about Margaret Atwood— Peggy, as she called her—that most of us did not know and also insights into related reading so that we could have more context about this particular book."

Another friend, Sylvia, subscribed to a monthly book club lecture series by a local retired college instructor who rented out a church basement for these meetings: "It was great. Really, the best part was that I love to read good new books, but there are so many coming out every day that I never know where to start in choosing one. The lecture series may have felt a bit too much like school in some ways, but at least it gave me the guidance I needed to stay an informed reader."

Always Be Prepared: Thinking Ahead to Your First Meeting

Whether you decide to have a member-led or an expert-led group, or alternate between the two, someone should at least prepare the following for the first meeting of a particular author:

* Some biographical information about the author, including nationality, age when the book was written, education and, if possible, related historical material. The Internet or your local library, or even something as simple as an entry from the encyclopedia, can be of great help here. As you will see in the "Sample Readings" later in this book, gathering and discussing biographical information on the author can be a great aid in getting any conversation started, since it is often just too tempting to relate the circumstances of the author's life to the work she or he has produced.

* Bibliographical information, including what else the author has written, reviews of the book in question and comments made by the author in interviews or in other writings. Many contemporary authors have given interviews that have been published, the most complete and insightful collections being those gathered in the pages of *The Paris Review* and later collected in book form by editor George Plimpton. Historical writers can be researched by reading their other books and published letters, or critical articles about them.

* A few sample questions or comments to kick-start the discussion: "I found the language in Michael Ondaatje's *The English Patient* poetical and very moving. I'd like to read the following brief passage to get us talking about how he tells his story" or "I think Margaret Laurence's *The Stone Angel* can be better understood with the following words she said in an interview just after the book came out..."

As you look through "Sample Readings," you will find many more potential discussion topics to get your group's conversation started.

Is You Is, or Is You Ain't?

It is important, even at this early stage of reading this very book you have in your hands, to talk about what a book club is *not*, which may even provide more helpful insights than defining what it is supposed to be.

* The book club is not a school or a classroom, where one person lectures or teaches the others. It is an adult interchange of ideas and insights. Book clubs feed off the juices of all members. Allowing one person to dominate or pontificate has been the downfall of many a group. Keep the form democratic and ensure that everyone participates at her or his comfort level. Everyone in the club should be inspiring everyone else.

* It does not have final exams or papers. You may want to prepare a few notes or you may encourage members to lead the discussion for that day. But don't get this mixed up with assignments that create more angst than enjoyment.

* It is not a therapy session, although, as in the rest of life, there may very well be a therapeutic tenor to comments made and ideas proposed. When the discussion heads too far off on a personal tack, try to nudge it gently back on to the path by referring back to specific elements of the text. There is no need to worry, though, unless things really get out of hand. After all, many writers have used books for therapeutic reasons. They are just good at objectifying it and making it more universal. As someone once said, James Joyce battled his whole life to get away from religion, while W. B. Yeats spent his whole life battling to get closer to some form of religion. If such struggles were good enough for them, they're good enough for us more humble readers.

✳ It is not a place to show off your erudition or turn a deaf ear to others' comments, however ill-phrased or ill-informed those comments may be. Save that attitude for the annoying person at the office who won't stop asking you "so how was your weekend?"

✳ As to the direction of your club's readings, there does not have to be a specific thematic or chronological order. Why not jump from a memoir to a contemporary novel to poetry to history? Negotiating the way from one form of information to another can be disconcerting at first but can lead to some truly inspiring insights. All these areas of human endeavour complement and enrich each other. Arrive prepared with questions just in case no conversation happens, but be prepared not to even look at them if the conversation takes on a life of its own. In other words, be organized but flexible, ready for a structured discussion but also to allow the discussion to be as chaotic and free-flowing as the members of your group are inspired to make it.

On Your Way

Later in this book we suggest a list of 100 fiction and 100 non-fiction books to get you going. For now, before you start reading your first book, keep in mind the few hints and suggestions we've offered here. A bit of organization up front can make or break your group down the road. The monthly meeting of your book club, formed by you and a few friends, can be the most supportive and stimulating event of your month. But, as is so often the case, it can also lead to divisiveness and hard feelings if not handled with some discretion and foresight.

In brief, within a few broad parameters, a book club is what you make it. We have both been in a variety of book clubs and although there are differences among them, there are also a few basics about all book clubs. They all have a sense of shared passion and mutual sympathy. They gather together people who love to read (let's face it: after all is said and done and read, what more interesting person is there than one who loves to read?). They are all rewarding, in creative, intellectual and social ways. And, above all, they are a lot of fun.

Let's Give Them
Something to
Talk About:

Why Start a
Book Club?

Canada has had writers, and has them now,
and they have not been trivial in their achievement.
What Canada needs is serious, demanding readers.

ROBERTSON DAVIES, *THE WELL-TEMPERED CRITIC*

The Best-Laid Plans

If you build it, they will (well, there's always a chance they might not) come. No matter how committed you are to getting your book club started or to sprucing up your stagnant book club, no matter how inspiring and fun you know it is going to be, it ain't going to be easy. As Robert Burns might have said if he were alive today, often the best-laid plans of mice and men and women sometimes still won't keep a book club afloat.

Too many broken obligations, too much lost potential, too many co-workers looking at each other skeptically in the hallway, not mentioning the decline of their group, attest to the fact that even the most promising book club has some likelihood of...failing. Though there are no statistics on the subject, we speculate from our own experiences that more than half of book clubs started do not survive to celebrate their first anniversary. You might as well get married or start a restaurant—the stats may be more favourable.

If you're going to give this idea a try, and if you really expect the experiment to enjoy any success, there are many simple and practical things you can do. But at this stage, it's also important to be aware of the difficulties and pitfalls of the whole process. Ignorance is bliss, but ignorance of the possible problems won't do you any good when setting up your club.

Your leadership skills and your ability to work well with others may be seriously called into question. (And don't forget, in theory, you are doing this all for *fun*, as an *escape* from the responsibilities of work!) People will from time to time disappoint you. You will sometimes end up feeling as though you have placed a burden on some people, even though you really began by trying to bring something special and unique into their lives. There will be moments when you seriously question why you bothered in the first place.

Our friend Annette, who was the founding member of a short-lived book club, commented on this issue for us: "It's funny. I started the book club in the first place because I really thought that people wanted it. At least that's what they told me. They were gung-ho. Why else would I have bothered?

"But right from the start all that I heard was one excuse after another. This person didn't have time to read any of the books because her in-laws were in town and she had to take them shopping every night. And that one couldn't attend any of the meetings because the workload was unbearable. In the end, of the twelve people who originally signed on, maybe four or five would show up regularly after the first three months. What kind of discussions could we have, really? And it was demoralizing. We tried all kinds of different strategies to give new life or momentum to the group, but with no luck. Five months later, we just stopped scheduling any meetings. It was just easier that way."

In our modern society, one doesn't have to look very far to find any number of reasons why *not* to start a book club. It is hard enough to get a group of people together for a game of bridge, or to get three friends to agree on a particular movie on a Friday night, never mind get them to attend a scheduled meeting every two weeks where each individual in attendance is expected to have read several hundred pages of a text! It is a lot to ask of people. It is time consuming. It is not for everyone, no matter how great the initial enthusiasm. This awareness, harsh though it be, is as good a place as any to begin.

Suddenly, your best intentions have become an imposition for all involved, and you are ready to throw your hands up in frustration. Is it worth the headache? Is it worth the stress?

It will help, before you approach the first potential members of your group, if you have a clear understanding of why you are doing this, and what a book club could offer you and other members. How did the idea first occur to you? Is it something that you have been thinking about for a long time, or did you recently notice the current fad and want to see what all the fuss is about? Do you remember the great discussions you used to have in high school or university about books and want to recapture a little of that magical intellectual stimulation? Is the daily grind making you yearn for some kind of social interaction? If you haven't sorted out all these questions, then it may be too easy to give up once you hit that first resistance.

If you can't answer these questions, then maybe you will realize that you are better off not starting your group at all. If that is the case, then *Build a Better Book Club* will have just saved you several months of frustration, and buying this book may be the best money you've spent in a long time. But if you have come up with satisfactory answers, or don't want to take "No, that's the night 'Ally McBeal' is on" for an answer, then it's time to start thinking about what the book club will add to your life.

Workin' Nine to Five

When we look closely enough at these negatives, it becomes evident why book clubs are becoming increasingly necessary to maintaining balance in our lives. Within our normal nine-to-five regimen, every moment is allotted to some duty or responsibility that we think is absolutely crucial to our survival. If we don't get the laundry done tonight, we tell ourselves, then it will never get done. If we don't watch "Friends" or "Melrose Place" or CNN this week, then we won't have a clear idea of who's zoomin' who, locally or internationally. Every moment is part of the routine: our morning coffee at 8:30a.m., our evening bath at 10:30p.m. Our two-week vacation arrives every six months, after which we return, hopefully renewed, for another six-month grind.

So what's the problem? Well, if the problem isn't self-evident by now, maybe there isn't a problem at all. Go back to the routine that we've just described. Enjoy. Have a nice life.

But to most people it will be apparent that this system of life, this routine—standing at this endless conveyor belt, tightening bolts like Charlie Chaplin in *Modern Times*—leaves little time or space for personal growth, introspection or meaningful social interaction. Our routines are so strict and comfortable, so easy to accept, that we may be in danger of losing our ability to evaluate our own lives. The only information that reaches us is fed by the media or Hollywood sensationalism. How or when are we supposed to step back and see ourselves, see our worlds, with the keen critical eye we once had before the world started to move so quickly?

We are losing our ability to seek out new ideas and to share our reactions to those ideas in a meaningful way. The more comfortable or strict our routines, the less room there is for the kind of growth that comes from the discovery of enduring writings. Our local newspaper's discussions of the latest political scandal simply cannot provide as much insight as the work of a writer who is attempting to create a text of lasting significance. Without the worlds created in books, how are you supposed to know the real world? How is your world going to have the chance to unfold?

Stop This Ride, I Want to Get Off

Now more than ever, we need something in our life that is going to allow us to step off that conveyor belt for a short while each day or week, to think, and to begin to get more in touch with our own personal progress. Where television numbs us with simplicity, the written word challenges and elevates us. Where television blares at us as we sit passive and unstimulated on the couch, a book engages us, draws us in, forces us to become involved in the process as readers and interpreters. Reading the local newspaper, newsmagazine or popular book is, in many respects, a healthier exercise than watching even the best educational television; the physical action of reading itself—the commitment, the process of integrating words on the page and anticipating narrative, the act of holding the publication in your hands, moving your eyes repetitively back and forth in the act of discovery—is far more stimulating than the act of watching and being told. Reading is a workout for the brain; television is most often an attack on the senses. As the eminent French sociologist Pierre Bourdieu states, television emphasizes "the sensational and the spectacular"; it poses "a serious danger for all the various areas of cultural production—for art, for literature, for science, for philosophy and for law."

The book club not only inspires members to re-introduce introspection into their lives, but brings all interpreters together periodically to share their thoughts and reflections, elevating each other in the process of creating a tapestry of ideas. In the words of our friend Judy: "Before I joined a book club, it was just easy not to read. Month after month, year after year, I never got around to it, even though I would read the book review section in the local paper, walk through bookstores, even buy books that looked interesting. Sometimes, we just need that little push. I don't think that people should have a problem admitting that."

The remainder of this chapter is divided into some of the reasons why individuals might be inspired to start or join a book club. Of course, these divisions are artificial. No one will want to be part of a book club for only social or only intellectual or only spiritual reasons. These reasons will co-exist, and sometimes may even be indistinguishable from each other. But it may help to understand each of these reasons separately. Once you understand why you are taking the initiative to start your club, you may find it easier to define your club's objectives more effectively.

Coffee Talk

One of the most basic reasons for wanting to start or join a book club is to add a little more social interaction to your life. Even if you haven't really enjoyed a life-long relationship with books, even if you're not quite sure that you are necessarily a "book person," even if you're not sure if this is the perfect time in your life to commit yourself to 300 extra pages of reading per month, almost everyone would like an excuse to go out and chat with five or ten or twenty friendly faces every month. As our book club friend Jon puts it: "Let's face it, I'm not going to turn down the chance to have a few laughs with some friends. What am I missing on a normal week night—a few more reruns? A few more gossipy phone calls?"

When our book club began, one of the invited members continued to attend religiously but obviously had little or no interest in reading the chosen material. Meeting after meeting, she would show up at the bar, order a big plate of fries and a beer, gossip about her friends and co-workers, and sit silent when the discussion of the book was taking place. "I didn't really think that I had time to actually read the novels," she confessed to us one day, "but I felt as though these meetings were a great chance to hang out with all the people who I like but who I rarely get to see in any kind of social setting."

Of course, this situation is not necessarily ideal, since those members who do make the effort don't necessarily want people around who are there only to socialize. In fact, the more this friend continued to attend and hear the rewarding discussions that were going on around her, the more her curiosity grew, and eventually she became one of the most committed readers in the group. "Suddenly, I realized how much I was missing," she said, "and I realized that if something is important enough, you can find the time for it, no matter how busy you are. Since I started really joining in, I have found that reading has given me so much pleasure.

"No matter how much the pressures of the day get to me, there's always an escape into another world of ideas at the end of it. I've made my book club reading my bedtime reading. I know it sounds like a cliché but it really has given me something to look forward to, no matter what happens in the normal workday. I pretty much know who I'll be seeing every day, what we'll be discussing, what issues we'll be tackling. I mean, how many times can I answer the question, 'How ya doing?' But my book club books always hold a new surprise at the end of each day."

You may want to tell your family and friends that your time with your book club is only for intellectual stimulation, but you should never underestimate the value of it as a social setting. Whatever your reasons for starting your book club, it can only be a good thing that, every once in a while, it gives you the chance to get out of the house, to put the issues of your life behind you, to go someplace where the usual demands are not put upon you. Another member of our book club, Sarah, was happy to articulate this point: "Every day it's the same thing for me. Work until 5:30p.m., get home, make supper for the kids, make sure that their homework is done and that they get to bed on time. Watch the same reruns on television and then go to sleep feeling as though there was never really one second for me to really find any meaningful time for myself.

"The book club gives me that time just that once every two weeks. It's time for myself. Just that once, I can forget all those other pressures and demands. The world doesn't fall apart just because I've given myself this luxury. In the end, everybody is better off for it, because I can put so much more into the usual routine knowing that this escape is there for me. The next day, I'm renewed. I can help the kids with their homework without losing my patience. I can get some work done at home without feeling overwhelmed and I can watch television without feeling as though I'm wasting my time—all because I've given myself this one little...indulgence. Just ask my kids! They'll back all this up!"

Indeed, the fact that your book club exists for intellectual stimulation makes the social dynamic even more interesting. Within the confines of the book club meeting, you can interact with people in a different way than you do anywhere else. In what other setting can you challenge or confront people in such a socially acceptable way? In this one place, the more you challenge, the more you argue (constructively, of course), the greater your contribution. Let's face it, there is not one of us who wouldn't enjoy the opportunity to argue our ideas through once in a while, but the way that our society is set up, we are made to feel as though we always have to be polite and diplomatic. In your book club, you are encouraged to say what's on your mind, because there's no right and wrong; there is only the common desire to share your own personal impression of the book.

Perhaps the healthiest thing about the social dynamic of the book club is that it gives us the opportunity to cease, if only for a short while, playing the various roles that we each have to play in life. At work, we must be industrious and tactful. At home, we must be wife or husband or significant other, parent or child, sibling or room-mate. In our book clubs, there is the opportunity to leave all that behind; if you have a point to make, you can make it as passionately or as quietly as you choose. It's your decision. Best of all, you don't have to worry about being "wrong." Your opinion, your reading, is as valid as anyone else's.

According to Norman, a member of a book group started between co-workers: "It's great to be able to debate novels with the people from around the office. In the hallway, we just say the usual clichés, 'How's it going?' or 'Thank God it's Friday!' At meetings we say, 'Do you have those figures yet?' or 'It's time to draw up next year's strategic plan.' But at our book club, we can look at each other and say, 'No, I don't agree with that reading. Here is how I see it...' or 'How can you say that when in the very next chapter that same character obviously has a change of heart?' And the next day we can just go back to the same office clichés as before, but at least for a short time, we were all somehow...humanized."

Back to School

As rewarding and vital as this social interaction is, one of the most important reasons why any of us would be inspired to start or join a club must be the need to add a little intellectual stimulation to our lives. Each of us can remember back to the days of grade school, high school, college or university, to the moment when we were first exposed to a new novel, play, poem or written historical account and suddenly, thanks to the vision and insight of the writer, so many of the perplexities of life became clear. We couldn't wait to hear what our teachers and classmates had to say—we couldn't wait to run to the local library to see what else that writer had written. These are the moments we sometimes yearn to return to, though once we are out of school, they seem so far in the past, so difficult to reclaim.

We attend school until a certain age, and during that time we have teachers who fill our heads with information and facts and hopefully certain skills for coping or thinking or doing. "What I want is, facts. Teach these boys and girls nothing but Facts. Facts alone are wanted in life. Plant nothing else, and root out everything else." It's not quite as bad as this memorable scene from Charles Dickens' *Hard Times*, but it sometimes seems that way. And then, once we have reached that age, we are given a task and we spend most of the remainder of our lives completing or repeating that task, whether it is welding or adding up numbers or selling something or even filling the minds of other young people with facts and skills. But no one ever explains to us why, once we have reached that magical age, we have to stop learning what to think and how to think. Perhaps, out of necessity, we stop remembering how it felt to learn something new, to enjoy that moment of discovery. Yet the feeling never really leaves us; it just lies dormant, waiting to be awakened again.

Of course, anyone can read alone and learn something from reading. And most of us do so, at least sporadically. But without the advantage of your book club, it may be too easy simply to let it slide, day after day, week after week. And your book club also offers each member the unique opportunity not only to learn from the books, but to learn from each other as well. "I always loved to read," said our friend Maureen, who recently joined a book club with some of her neighbours, "but the problem was, I would read the book, then I would put the book down or return it to the library, and that would be that. Now, when I have the opportunity to talk about the book with the seven or eight other members who show up to each book club meeting, I feel like I'm experiencing the book over and over again. It becomes much harder to forget the book at this point. Everyone in the group has a different opinion, and every opinion makes me see the book in a different way. Instead of the book just being forgotten on the shelf, it comes to life, again and again, in the course of the discussion."

Each member benefits from what the others have to say, and each enjoys the advantage of allowing his or her own thoughts to develop as well. "And sometimes I don't know what's going to come out when I start giving my reaction to a book," continues Maureen. "Let's say that we are reading one of our chosen books, *A Lesson Before Dying* by Ernest J. Gaines, and someone starts talking about the politics of the book. Well, the truth is that maybe I hadn't thought about this topic up until now, because I was reading the novel more for the human drama and the history of racism in the South. I wasn't really thinking, before that, of how the political situation of the town where the story is set has influenced the action of the story.

"So, in order to respond, I have to search my mind for some impressions, and suddenly I'm talking and my thoughts are being formed as I'm listening to my own voice, I can tell that there are some great ideas coming out. Everyone is listening. Some are even taking notes on the inside cover of their copies of the book. It is a great feeling, knowing that my ideas are taking form. Knowing that I'm making a difference to the conversation. It might not be a grand insight, but to our book club it seems like it is."

The book club also allows individuals the opportunity to be exposed to books that they might not normally have sought out themselves. Sometimes in life we allow ourselves to fall into an established pattern, and it becomes harder and harder to break out of it. Someone who reads primarily romance novels might find it hard to force themselves to pick up one of James Joyce's books to see what all the fuss is about. A die-hard businessman might not normally allow himself the opportunity to put down Donald Trump's *The Art of the Deal* long enough to enjoy the rich world of a novel like Louisa May Alcott's *Little Women*.

In a book club, books are most often chosen democratically, and members, eventually, cannot help but read "uncharacteristic" books, which is often their most meaningful and rewarding read in years. This experience allows members to expand their horizons, taking in new ideas, stretching their imaginations beyond the tight restrictions of their world.

It is easy to see how this "restricted" reading pattern might hold true for, say, a lawyer who sees John Grisham books as particularly relevant, or for a computer specialist for whom the latest science fiction best seller might seem more appropriate than Martha Stewart's book on planning the superior wedding. In fact, we all experience the same limitations, whether we are aware of it or not.

We know one university professor who specializes in nineteenth-century British literature and who has belonged to a very healthy book club for more than a decade. One might ask why a person who gets paid to read and to think about what she is reading and to lecture on her thoughts would want to belong to a book club. Wouldn't she rather spend her evenings playing tennis or vegging in front of the television or doing...basically anything other than reading more books and talking about them?

"The book club is of vital importance to me and the relative health of my mind," she told us. "Within my field, there are of course many great writers and works, both in poetry and in prose. And there is always something new to discover within that world. And there is always a new book coming out on Byron or

Shelley or any of the other writers in my field that I have to read, and sometimes I am even the writer of these books or articles or conference papers.

"That is my work and my livelihood. But often I need an escape from that too. Sure, sometimes the members of my group vote for us to read and discuss a book that most of my colleagues in the English department would consider 'trashy.' Sometimes I'm even self-conscious about bringing one of those books to work, thinking that my colleagues might ridicule me if they see me with a book that is less 'serious' than what I'm supposed to be reading. I mean, imagine a football player coming to work with a copy of *The Celestine Prophecy*. That's how I feel sometimes when I have to carry around something like *Men Are from Mars, Women Are from Venus* or *Chicken Soup for the Soul*, even in the subway on my way into work.

"Okay, so I'm being a little facetious, but the truth is that the books I read because of my book club are often the books that open me up most. They allow me to be in touch with what people are thinking about today, not just what they were thinking about 150 years ago. They allow me to take in new ideas, to make these new ideas part of my life. I think that the most important thing in all this is that these new books and new ideas allow me to come back to my own work with new insight and energy.

"And you should see the look in my students' eyes when I let them know that I've actually read a Michael Creighton novel. It opens connections between me and the world that is happening now. It is fun to catch them off guard, or to use a reference to a more contemporary novel in order to show them the relevance of a much older work."

The point that all of our book club friends are making, in one way or another, is simple: the process of acquiring new information, of expanding one's horizons through the experience of reading, of keeping up with the latest ideas or reaching back in time to get in touch with some that may at first seem outdated should never end. As William Ellery Channing said in 1838: "It is chiefly through books that we enjoy intercourse with superior minds...God be thanked for books, they are the voices of the distant and the dead, and make us heirs of the spiritual life of past ages." The only thing we would add to that quotation is that the current age also is full of superior minds and some pretty great writing, too.

Many people have books in their lives, but without the advantage of the book club they too easily can get stuck in an established groove, or allow the patterns of their reading to fade away too often. The book club opens us up, forces us to expand not only what we read but also, and perhaps more importantly, how we read, and the degree of insight that we bring with us to the experience.

Getting in the Spirit

In addition to the social and intellectual motivations for belonging to a book club, there are reasons that are less easily defined but, in many ways, more important. These we will call the spiritual reasons. Of course, loosely defined, there are spiritual rewards to be found both in the social and in the intellectual aspects of the book club as well. And the spiritual rewards of being part of a book club inevitably vary from person to person. Still, there are some general aspects of the spiritual dimension of the book club that are worth exploring.

First, we are convinced that there is a great deal of personal growth that can result from the book club experience (otherwise we would not be writing this book). Regardless of the outcome of your participation in a book club, you can learn a great deal both from the books you are reading and from the points of view of the other members of the group. The importance of this cannot be overstated. Each time that you read a book you walk away with a particular impression. If you hear one other person's impression, you not only experience another reading of the book, but you also experience how radically different another person's perception of the world can be. If you go through this process with ten other people, you are seeing how very differently each of these people can experience the world. You are opening up your perception again and again. In a sense you are reading the book many times over and seeing the world through many different sets of eyes. This type of intellectual and social interaction cannot help but expand your own naturally restricted horizon, make you more understanding, give you more options in terms of how you may see and experience literature and phenomena. This is personal growth in its purest form—broadening your perspective to include as many others as possible, to share your own and to integrate those of others.

A book club gives you the personal space that you need in order to develop (or to continue to develop) your sense of self, independent of the pressures of life. This is not to say that it is a magic formula for solving all the stressful problems or issues around you, but it is one option that is available to you. It may not work, but with so many possibilities (from the very simple and non-committal Internet discussion group to the fully developed, regularly scheduled book club meetings), it may be worth a try if you are feeling that your life is lacking that extra, perhaps evasive dimension beyond the daily routine.

As children we let the mysterious, the imaginative and the spiritual into our lives and into the way we see everything around us. Children learn through the imagination before they learn through facts. Just ask any child about imaginary friends or about the stories he or she is constantly making up and sharing with others. It's a way of life and appreciating the things around us that perhaps we let slip away too easily. As Ralph Waldo Emerson said not so long ago, "Great men are they who see that spiritual is stronger than any material force, that thoughts rule the world." Reading can help us recapture some of this innate and expansive view of ourselves and the world.

Never Talk
to Strangers:

The Social
Dynamic of
Your Book Club

I have always depended on the kindness of strangers.

TENNESSEE WILLIAMS, *A STREETCAR NAMED DESIRE*

Opposites Attract—Finding the Right People for Your Book Club

The most important aspect of creating a successful book club, or joining an existing book club, is finding the right people to create the perfect dynamic. This is accomplished by inviting or joining people whom you know to be agreeable (which, of course, is extremely important), and in finding the right mix of people.

When we were invited to join a book club with some people at work, the experience led us to believe that just about everyone had been invited (how else would we have made the cut?). When we showed up to the first meeting, we just assumed that the group was composed of those people who had decided to accept the invitation.

We were wrong. There was nothing random about the grouping of people who had been asked to attend, nor should there have been. Our friend Debra, who had initiated the group, had carefully chosen the people whom she felt would constitute the best and most dynamic collection of club members: "I remember when I made the decision to start the book club, I kind of felt as though, in the interest of fairness, I had some kind of obligation to invite everyone in the office," she recently admitted. "But the more I thought about it, the more I realized that this kind of democratic approach would immediately doom the club. I didn't want people who I knew would just be enthusiastic but who wouldn't have anything interesting or critical to say about the books. Nor did I want people who would just hate everything, without really having anything to back up their opinions. And then there were all those people who I knew would be too lazy or busy to read the books, and would just be wasting everyone's time.

"I guess that what I'm saying is that I quickly realized that the book club, at least at the beginning, couldn't be a democracy. It was a sort of dictatorship. I was, for lack of a better word, the dictator. And the success hinged on my judgement. I think that this is the only way these things could work. It's a lot of responsibility for the one or two people doing the choosing, but the way I see it, at least *someone* is taking responsibility."

Mix 'n' Match

There are many decisions that must be made before you sit down to write a list of invited members. Some of the decisions require some guess work on your part. For instance, you have to try to anticipate who, among your group of acquaintances, will have the most staying power, and will not be inclined simply to fade away after one or two meetings. Stay away from people you know to be into fads who may lose their enthusiasm too quickly. If you have a friend with a basement full of unused exercise equipment, disco balls, exotic fish that have perished from starvation, and a library of diet and self-help books, then this may not be the model candidate to appear on your member list.

But the first and perhaps most important decision is how you want your group to interact. Some people may want to use the book club more as a place for a social outing than anything else. These people will probably want to invite people they know who are the most fun in a social setting. There is nothing wrong with this; if it works for you, have a good time.

We know about many book clubs where the book is just an excuse for a bunch of friends to get together in a bar and chat about the day's events. These "book discussions" usually sound something like this:

"Has everyone read this month's book?"

"Um...most of it..."

"Yeah...some!"

"And so, what did we think?"

"Good..."

"Not bad..."

"I liked the first chapter. It seemed funny."

"These chips are really good."

"Did you hear what John said to Cindy at the photocopier today?"

"That guy's a jerk. I dunno what Carol sees in him."

"Yeah, but c'mon. Is Carol any better?"

And so on and so on. You get the picture. Sometimes the book is not necessarily the important thing. And if the club gives you the chance to read one or two decent books over the course of a year, you can consider yourself lucky. The point is, if this is the kind of club that you want, or the kind of club that you want to be part of, then make sure that you invite the people with the juiciest gossip, and make sure that you save yourself the seat next to that person!

Mensa Members—Down the Hall and to the Right

Of course, for most people, the point of the book club is to talk about books, so they want to find a group of people who can sustain a discussion at the level they feel would be most beneficial. This does not necessarily mean looking for a group of English professors, all of whom will arrive armed with their published deconstructive reading of each sentence of the book under discussion. Good discussions about books are not always academic discussions about books. You can have a great book talk without it taking the form of duelling arguments by world-renowned experts. You just have to know what tone you want for your group before you can find the people who are most likely to strike the right note.

There are many possibilities to choose from in determining the tone of your club. You may want to gather a group of individuals who you know will always generate a good argumentative discussion. Your choices, therefore, would probably include people from many different backgrounds and, perhaps more importantly, you would invite people with different political orientations. There is nothing like intentionally gathering together a group of six or seven liberal thinkers with a group of six or seven conservatives. Left to their own devices, this group as a whole would choose the first topic that came up from current events, say a prominent politician's philandering or healthcare spending, and they would be off to the races. Their debate would follow a fairly standard path. The liberals would assume the position of their political party, and the conservatives would offer a consistent position to whatever party represented them in the last election. Nothing new or interesting in that debate. Just another excuse to get red in the face and go home frustrated yet again.

But what if, instead of debating the same old points that are repeated *ad nauseam* on television, this group were thrown together with a copy of, say, *The Adventures of Huckleberry Finn* to debate. Perhaps the political positions of the members of the group would still be consistent, but it would be a great deal more demanding for people to defend their positions, because suddenly the issues would be different, and the script wouldn't be quite as standardized (when was the last time that any of us heard Jean Chrétien or any other North American politician offering his opinions on Mark Twain, or any writer, for that matter?).

In this case, someone in the group might suggest that an interesting aspect of *Huck Finn* is that it calls into question the issue of society's responsibility toward the parentless child both in the southern U.S. in the late nineteenth century and today. The conversation might move toward an understanding of how this complex issue is handled by Twain within the context of the novel. Then the group might extend that argument to its own society. At this point, the conversation would be much more interesting than if the group were discussing the topic independent of the novel, because the novel and the character of Huck himself would provide a backdrop for the political positions of the group members. If, for example, a member of the group were to put forth the point of view that society has little obligation toward this child, particularly if the child were considered delinquent and resistant toward any kind of institutionalization, then other members of the group would have to gesture back toward Huck himself, and demand to know how that political position reflects back on that character and his story. It becomes far more challenging to stick to a particular party line when that line has to be pointed back relentlessly toward the work under discussion.

Anyone Here Need a Hug?

Of course, heated arguments are not everyone's cup of tea, and if you are looking to create a group that is softer around the edges, then it won't help to invite your favourite Pat Buchanan clone and your favourite Jesse Jackson clone and stick them in a room together to debate *The Autobiography of Malcolm X.* Some people want to create a group that provides a safer and more nurturing space. In this case, you will probably want to begin by choosing people who have more consistent points of view both politically and in other ways.

What you are aiming for in the "safe" book club is a group atmosphere where all participants can say pretty much whatever is on their mind without any fear of being cut down and made to feel stupid. This, we have found over the years, is the one thing that may keep many people away from the book club (or class-room or social group or whatever), or may keep them from enjoy-ing the group. As one of our fellow book club members put it recently: "Like almost everybody, I feel belittled from time to time. My boss...well, let's not talk about him. The snooty waiter at the corner greasy-spoon near my house does it to me. My mother-in-law does it to me. Let's face it, I ain't going to go looking for yet another stressful place. If I didn't feel as though anything that I said in the book club was valid, and I mean *anything*, I would just pick up and leave. What do I need more stress in my life for?"

Obviously, one way in which you can ensure a certain comfort level in your group is to avoid inviting people you know to have a track record of attacking others who express opinions that run counter to their own. One person capable of humiliating a club member can keep the whole group quiet or, worse, prevent others from showing up. Remember, it is your choice whom to invite. If you want a conflict-oriented group, then go looking for conflict-oriented people. But if you are looking to create a compatible and harmonious group, then members should check their killer instinct at the door or stay home.

Your choice of books also helps create the right social atmosphere. If you want your club members to feel comfortable, then choose reading material that will not offend them or put them on the defensive. If you are looking for conflict, challenge, confrontation, then pick up Howard Stern's *Private Parts* and invite people to express their opinion on what they think of the author's unique sense of tact.

Even though conflict may work for some people, it will inevitably raise the level of anxiety and discomfort among members. If your club is going to be a safe one, start with classics like *Little Women* or *Pride and Prejudice*. Focus on the positive. Allow the members of your club to begin the discussion by talking about what it is in these books that appeals to them most. Start on the intellectual level, and try to avoid bringing people into the discussion on an emotional level, especially if some of the more controversial topics begin to arise. If, while discussing *Pride and Prejudice*, someone raises the issue of the treatment of women in nineteenth-century England, then be prepared to let people speak, but try not to allow them to alienate anyone else in the group.

Boys to the Left, Girls to the Right

Perhaps the most important consideration in pondering the social dynamic of your book club will be the gender mix of your club's members. Somehow, the book club seems to have emerged as the last club on Earth where it is entirely appropriate to start out by saying something like: "Sorry, this club is for women/men only." And many book clubs define themselves accordingly, where it is not only necessary to choose a group of individuals with common interests or common goals or from the same culture or neighbourhood, it is also necessary that all the individuals chosen be of the same gender.

Although we do not have any specific statistics on the subject, from our own observations we would guess that, at present, over 50 percent of the book clubs that exist are exclusively made up of women or men. And we would further speculate that of those groups, probably three quarters are entirely female. However, the tradition of men-only book discussion groups extends far back. For instance, many of the groups that are now exclusively male college fraternities originally formed as book groups.

It would be inconceivable today to think of a golf club that was allowed so narrowly to restrict its membership, or a health club or a bridge club or anything else. So why, when it comes to the book club, can people restrict their groups with such impunity?

The answer to this question is complex, but it is also worth pondering as a way of gaining some additional insight into the phenomenon and appeal of the book club. The book club exists to allow individuals the (sometimes rare) opportunity in their weekly or monthly routines to enjoy some intellectual, spiritual and social stimulation. It is, therefore, a space away from the pressures of daily life. Also worth considering is the phenomenon of the same-sex book club that took form completely on its own; no one set it down in stone as a good or advisable way of commencing a book discussion group. Nor is it our intention, in this book, to advocate either the one-sex book group or the mixed book group as preferable to the other. The question, then, is whether the predominance of one-sex book clubs, especially in light of the fact that these groups have taken form on their own, suggests that many people simply regard the presence of members of the other sex as an impediment to the full enjoyment or experience of this intellectual/social event. The answer, for whatever reason, seems to be a resounding yes.

We can only speculate on why this is the case. Perhaps it has something to do with the fact that, for whatever reason, people perceive members of the other sex as potentially more judgemental, particularly on an intellectual level, and are therefore less inclined to blurt out their responses simply and freely when members of the opposite sex are present. A friend of ours who has belonged to a females-only book group for almost a decade puts it this way: "It's not that I am afraid to express my intellectual opinions in front of men. My husband would be happy to tell you how often I feel the need to be opinionated with him! It's not even that I sometimes wouldn't rather have a man present to express a different opinion, especially when we are doing a novel where the male and the female characters have radically different points of view within the story. It's just that there is more of a feeling of community this way. Less competition, I guess. We are not always working together or saying the same thing, but we are always somehow on the same wavelength. I wouldn't feel more threatened if men were present. But I would feel less community. It is just our place, away, for a short while. Personally, I don't think that's asking too much."

It may be old-fashioned to admit, but sometimes people simply need the company of members of their own sex. One might think that the men would sit around talking about women and the women would sit around talking about men. But there is something much more serious and elemental in this equation.

If, for example, two one-sex book groups, one male, the other female, were discussing *The Great Gatsby*, the fact is that each group would bring to the experience different experiences and different perspectives, and the two groups would probably enjoy very different discussions, neither more nor less meaningful than the other. Each group, at some point, might focus on Jay Gatsby's love for Daisy. While the members of the male group might focus on her attractiveness to him in terms of what she offers him socially, the female group might gravitate toward the question of whether his attraction revolves around Gatsby's desire to own everything, and how Daisy is simply another possession for him to add to his collection. Both these discussions are entirely valid and can be very fruitful. Both would take any good book discussion group in extremely meaningful and worthwhile directions. The point is, however, that the two groups naturally have different interests, different backgrounds, different experiences, and they may simply want their insights to roll in directions that are more consistent with their points of view.

There are other, more practical reasons why same-sex book clubs might take form. First, it is often the case that men and women simply do not enjoy the same books. That is not to say that we are born liking different things. As we all know, these things are often conditioned: little boys are often encouraged to read books about hockey heroes, little girls to read books about errant knights and damsels in distress.

Maybe that is taking it a little far, and maybe it is time that we start rejecting these stereotypes, but our social conditioning is not an issue to be debated in a book about book clubs. What is important is the fact that by the time we reach a certain age, we do not always want to pick up the same books. Stick men and women together in the same group, and chances are everything will be fine, few people will feel terribly threatened by the presence of members of the opposite sex, everyone will have a fairly good time socially. But we have known of groups where this was the case and the fact still remained that the men became frustrated and bored when female members voted to read books like *Waiting to Exhale* and *Lives of Girls and Women* (unless of course they were particularly sensitive men), while the women in the group just couldn't relate to some of the choices that the men made, like *The Natural* or *Portnoy's Complaint* (unless they were particularly patient women). In these cases, the conversation often stalls around the question of why members of one sex don't like the book while the others do. Not very fruitful.

You Just Wouldn't Understand

A second practical reason why the same-sex book group might be appealing is that it is a social setting where individuals can potentially share thoughts not related to the book discussion that they might be uncomfortable sharing with members of the opposite sex. As one female friend described to us, "I know that the whole purpose of the club is to talk about books. Okay, I get it. But sometimes I go and, frankly, I'm really looking forward to the opportunity to bounce some of my issues off some other women. And I know that the other women are looking for the same thing. So, if my boss is hassling me, or my mother-in-law is calling too often, or I want to talk about an issue related to my kids, sometimes I'll wait for the book discussion to die down a little and then ask the rest of the members about some of these issues. Where else am I sure that I'm going to run into so many trusted women friends all at once? Sometimes, if I have an issue that needs to be discussed, I'll even wait for the meeting so that I can get some reaction from some fellow women before making any decisions."

As you begin to conceive of the social make-up of your club, you should consider the same-sex club carefully, because, for whatever reason, they have been known to be some of the healthiest book clubs around. Should you decide to go this route, then do so without making any apologies. The important thing is building a book club that works, not one that satisfies some code of proper, politically correct conduct. If you sense that, within the collection of your potential invitees, all members of one gender will make up the longest lasting and most productive possible group, then that is the group that you should create.

Can't We All Just Get Along?

As popular and successful as same-sex book groups have proven to be, you may make the choice of inviting individuals based upon your impression of their personalities, their intelligence, their sense of humour, their profession, but not their sex, and if you still end up with a same-sex book group or a group that is predominantly one sex or the other, then so be it. Or you may make a conscious decision to create a group that is as close as possible to a 50-50 split between the sexes. These choices, too, have some profound effects on the dynamic of your group that should be explored.

This problem manifests itself again and again in our own book club, which is made up of a mixed group. While our group has, on the whole, enjoyed a very positive history thus far, certain problems do pop up. At one meeting, it so happened that the majority of the male members were present, but many of the female members could not attend. This was also the meeting at which we were supposed to vote upon the book that was going to be read the following month. The male members present elected to read Jack Kerouac's classic book *On the Road*, a particularly masculine story of one individual's travels and exploration. At the subsequent meeting, the female members returned, and our Kerouac selection was vetoed so quickly that we hardly knew what hit us. Were we bitter? Well, let's just say that if you show up at one of our meetings one day and whisper the name Kerouac, you may still hear a few quiet grumbles from both sides of the gender barrier.

It is also the case that club members may feel uncomfortable talking on certain subjects in front of members of the opposite sex. A group of women could, for example, decide to read a book that deals with the experience of menopause. A group of men could decide together to read a book on the subject of impotence and the effects of Viagra. Let's face it, neither group will be able to have as good a conversation, or maybe even any meaningful conversation at all, in front of members of the opposite group. It is too embarrassing. While these are extreme examples, this kind of thing happens all the time in the mixed group. The mixed group does, at times, limit book choices and conversation topics.

Yet there is much to recommend the mixed group, as we know from our own experience in our own book club. Admittedly, it can be somewhat more threatening to say something on a particularly sensitive topic in front of members of the opposite sex, but most of the time it simply doesn't matter among mature adults, especially if the men and women in the group have been carefully chosen from the onset for their affable, easygoing nature.

And at the same time the presence of both men and women in the group often charges the atmosphere, and leads to some extremely spirited and worthwhile debate. Of course, members of different sexes may have different readings of different texts, but for some book clubs, this is not something to fear but to embrace. To a great extent, it depends on what you want for your group. Some groups, as we have already said, prefer the safer atmosphere, where predominantly uncontroversial texts will be discussed by members of the same sex. Now, we are not saying that the mixed book club has to get together each month to discuss the collected works of the Marquis de Sade or the "Whacking Off" chapter of *Portnoy's Complaint*, or even the latest book on coping with PMS, but even a Margaret Atwood novel can spark some interesting disagreement, where some men in the group may react harshly to her depictions of men as oppressors, where women may be inclined to agree with her identification of women as victims in our society. The ensuing discussions may be disturbing to some, but can also be very healthy and educational to others. It is always good to know, after all, what the other sex is thinking.

Another interesting dynamic is created by what we'll call "The Imbalance Club," where there may be a vast majority from one sex or another. If this happens, it is important not to allow the minority of women or men to feel threatened. If your club includes ten women and two men, for example, you really only have two choices: let the men say anything, or ask them to leave, because you just can't keep beating up on them time after time— they're just men, after all!

Size Matters

In one of the most memorable moments of the novel *The Great Gatsby*, a character attending one of Jay Gatsby's spectacular parties says to another character, "I like large parties, they're so intimate. At small parties, there isn't any privacy." Clearly, the size of your book club has an enormous effect on the social dynamic of the group, and you have to decide how large you want the meetings to be before you invite your first member.

As mentioned in the first chapter, we recommend that, in terms of creating an ideal social dynamic, the group be somewhere between eight and twelve people. This can be tricky, as you should always expect at least two or three members of your group not to show up to any given meeting, due to prior commitments.

The reason why we chose these numbers is simple: any fewer and there are not enough people to offer the variety of opinions that you may be looking for. Members should feel free to talk when they wish, and to listen when they wish, but if the club is too small (say, five people), each individual may feel too much pressure to contribute to the discussion all the time and the meetings may cease to be enjoyable. If you do choose to form a relatively small group, it may help if all members are particularly good and long-standing friends who are comfortable enough with one another to speak easily on any subject without any fear of the other members passing judgement.

And yet a large group can present you with some opposite problems. When there are too many people present, individuals in the group may begin to feel lost and overwhelmed by the numbers. If there are, say, twenty people present, then there may only be one or two opportunities for each person to speak at all over the course of an hour-long meeting, and people may feel that they are constantly interrupting when they want to contribute their opinion. When the book club is working at its best, club members should feel like they are caught up in the flow of the discussion, where sometimes the conversation moves into an area where they feel comfortable and they can simply jump in with a comment, and sometimes the conversation moves away from them, where they can simply sit back and learn something from their fellow members. The larger group often does not work this way. It may feel more like school, where the individual is further removed from the group because it is more difficult to contribute. This may be fine if there is one individual leading the discussion or even lecturing. But in most cases, members of the book club want to feel equal to every other member, and therefore their opinion on any given topic can be offered as freely as they wish any time they wish.

Forming too large a group may also make it difficult to find a venue for meetings, and your group may end up incurring the added expense of renting space.

Background Check

Although it is extremely important to create a club that includes the people with the right personalities and with the right gender mix in the right numbers, you may also find that the background that each individual brings to the group is equally important. This again will force you to make some difficult decisions. Do you want to include people who all work in the same industry or office? Do you want people who all reside in the same condo complex? Or individuals who all come from the same ethnic background? Our own group is constituted of individuals from the same office, which has its advantages (it is always easy to find a convenient place to meet) and its disadvantages (there are some natural limitations on the points of view that members bring to a reading of a text—sometimes it is nice to hear what people from other walks of life think). Also (with apologies to the members of our own book club), it would be nice if your book club would allow you to see some new faces at the end of the day.

The ethnic make-up of your group can also prove important. In our own group there are individuals from different ethnic backgrounds, which, as much as the mix of genders, makes for some very interesting debate. For example, one month, early in the club's history, we were discussing the novel *Martin Dressler: Tale of an American Dreamer*, by Edward Millhauser. The novel deals with the son of German immigrants who, for some reason, is driven to become one of the great entrepreneurs and builders in New York City at the turn of the century. One of the topics that we chose to debate was Martin Dressler's motivations for pushing himself to build so much so fast. Those members of the group who themselves were from groups identified as ethnic minorities argued that the answer to this question was obvious. Martin Dressler pushed himself because, as an outsider to this society, he had to work that much harder to establish himself, or to make this world conform to him. Those members who were not from ethnic minorities disagreed with this reading, and argued that Martin Dressler's outward actions were motivated by his psychosexual inward awakening. An extensive and healthy debate ensued in which neither group was right or wrong, but both defended their opinions effectively and were drawn further and further into the book as a result.

Strangers in the Night

In previous chapters, we talked about other kinds of book club options available to you other than getting a group of friends together in a room somewhere. These included surfing the Internet to find discussions of the book you happen to be reading or subscribing to a local series of lectures on a list of books. For each of these options there will, of course, be different social consequences.

Discussing books in an Internet chat room is probably the most radically different alternative available. What is interesting about this option is that, since you will probably never meet your fellow "group members," you have complete freedom to offer much more radical interpretations of the book under discussion than you may ever feel free to do when you are facing a group of friends. Another advantage is that, while your own "traditional" book club may be limited to people with backgrounds similar to your own, in the Internet book group, you may share your opinion of *Men Are from Mars, Women Are from Venus* with people from Sweden, the Bronx, South Africa, pretty much anywhere in the world. Through this experience, you can see how different people in various parts of the world have similar or different perceptions of the same book you are reading.

Unfortunately, Internet chat room discussions can very easily be ruined by one person, somewhere out there, writing purposely insulting things, and therefore souring the entire experience. Perhaps the lesson in this is that, ultimately, there is no replacement for real, face-to-face discussion.

Are You Talking to Me?

As for the local lecture series option, once again there are serious advantages and disadvantages. Besides the initial cost of subscribing, it is certainly a very convenient way to get a structured book-reading regimen into your life. Ideally, you are also assured an enlightening lecture on the book, which will then provide food for thought as you continue to think about the book in question. At the same time, this option will give you the chance to meet many new people around your town who, by virtue of the fact that they are also at this lecture, have interests similar to yours.

But many people will not necessarily want to be spoken to by a single person when they could, potentially, participate in an equal and democratic discussion around a table. This is not to say that, at the end of the lecture, you cannot or should not ask some questions about the book. But if there are also 100 other enthusiasts clamouring to ask their questions, then you may not stand much of a chance of having your opinion heard.

Some friends of ours have come up with a good alternative. Since they were not certain whether they could sustain an entire discussion on their own, five of them subscribe, together, to a local lecture series. They each read the book, attend the lecture, and then immediately proceed to a café to discuss the book and the lecture together. This option, they have found, works beautifully, since they are not lacking any discussion topics after the lecture, and there is no pressure on any one member of this mini-club if they have to miss an evening.

If the Shoe Fits

In terms of the social dynamic of the book club, the point is to find the situation that fits you best. But most importantly, remember that this is not school and it is not supposed to bring added pressure to your life. If you wish to speak often and freely, find a club that allows you to do so. If you wish to sit passively and listen, once again, there are many different clubs that allow you to participate on this level. In today's world, there are many options and alternatives available, so choose the group that lets you read and grow without bringing any added stress to your life.

Shakespeare,
Rattle and Roll:

Building
Your Book Club

*It would be a mistake to suppose that a book club
will just run itself by its own momentum.*

HENRY HOWARD HARPER,
THE FUNCTIONS OF THE BOOK CLUB, 1871

The Call of the Wild: Picking
the Right Books for Your Group

So you have read the first three chapters of this book, you have
carefully considered your reasons for starting a book club and the
many challenges that lie ahead of you, and you have decided that
it is worth the effort. We think you are right. We are also sure
that, once you get beyond the initial butterflies, it will all be very
much worth the effort. You get on the phone or you talk to people
over lunch or you put up a few signs around your neighbourhood
or at the office or the local library, and you carefully coax five or
ten or fifteen friends and colleagues into your basement on a

Monday night with promises of an evening of lively and inspired conversation.

They arrive, or at least most of them do, and each one takes a seat, glaring at you with that cross-armed, defensive, "okay, what's this all about?" posture. The conversation is apprehensive and anticipatory. Or, put another way, part excitement and part dread.

You are standing or sitting before them, at their bookish mercy. If you are not prepared for this moment, the first thought that will go through your head will be something like: "Okay...so...here I am...and there are you. Oh my God, what now?" And you can be guaranteed that their first thought will be: "I'm missing 'Melrose Place' for this? Well, I know where I'm not going to be next Monday!"

This is the crucial moment, and you had better be ready for it if your group is going to meet for a second time. But what does it mean to be "ready for it"? Well, in fact, most of the preparation should have come before this first meeting ever takes place. The most important thing to do before the first meeting is to figure out the right books for your group to discuss, or at least determine the common interests of the members and start to define the group based upon those interests. Let's face it, there is no point in creating a book club for the purpose of discussing books of epic poetry of the fifteenth century if no one in the group has any interest in poetry or the fifteenth century. At the same time, you don't want a group that will be so static that it can discuss books only about inner-city gardening or about baking better chocolate chip cookies.

In finding the right intellectual level for your group, there are many choices to be made, and these choices have a great deal to do with the personalities of the members of the group. It is always a good idea for people to vote on which books to read, but ultimately some order must be imposed. You can, for example, generate a list of ten books that everyone can vote on, using a variety of sources, including best-seller lists, the lists in the appendix to this book, university course lists (just call the English Department of your local college or university and ask for the reading list of the Introduction to Literature course), lists of other book clubs, lists culled from the bookshelves of your friends or neighbours, lists from the Internet, lists recommended by the staff at the local library, and so on. If none of this works, then simply consult the staff at your favourite bookstore. Most will be happy to give you all the time and help you want, especially if you mention you are a member of a book club (i.e., more sales are likely to result if the staff is friendly to you).

For our own book club, we prepared for the first meeting simply by pulling a list of recent award-winning books off the Internet and then voting on the first couple of books at the meeting. This worked fairly well, though we tried to choose books that no one had read and this lack of guidance eventually led to our choosing some less-than-satisfying books.

You also have to gauge the political and cultural sensitivities of the group. For example, because of their controversial nature and the chance for real fireworks in any discussion of them, *Lolita* by Vladimir Nabokov or *Backlash* by Susan Faludi may not be the best book for your group to begin with. *Lolita* is one of the most important books of the century and Nabokov is a great, if quirky, stylist. But an older man's relationship with a teenage girl may not be the sort of book to bring to your all-female group. Likewise, Faludi's book may be too political or too combative for members intent on reading escapist fiction.

You must be able to assess the levels of sensitivity (cultural, political, racial, etc.) of the members of your group. But these two books, and some of the others we mention in the lists included at the end of this book, may be exactly what your club needs if it starts to drag its heels a bit. In our experience, some of the best discussions revolve around controversial books. As one of our book club members recently said: "Personally, I hated *Martin Dressler: Tale of an American Dreamer,* but it certainly got me thinking. I haven't been so wound up about a book since my first year of university. And it really inspired some great conversations." Another friend had some trying times in her group when they read *The Color Purple*, by Alice Walker: "I don't know what there is *not* to love about the book," she told us "but there were a few people who were just bored by it. They couldn't get beyond Walker's use of language and therefore never really got engaged by the story. It was strange when we discussed the book. Most of the group was in awe of Walker's talent while a few sat around like bumps on a log."

In addition, you will have to decide if the people whom you have chosen would prefer only recent books, or if they would like to discuss classic books as well. Let's say you want to talk about racism. Would the members of your group prefer to read *Uncle Tom's Cabin* by Harriet Beecher Stowe or Oprah's latest selection off the best-seller list or both?

One of the tricky issues in defining your book club may be the choice between fiction and non-fiction. Some potential members may be distinctly unenthusiastic about reading anything except travel books, while others may be hooked on mystery novels. Navigating through these and other choices will demand diplomacy, tact or a great sales job.

Decisions, Decisions (Part One)

There are other basic decisions to make before or at the first meeting, which will be adjusted or adapted as your group continues to meet. They include, but are certainly not limited to, the following:

How Often Your Group Should Meet. There is no correct answer for this question, although in our experience, groups that meet every two or three weeks tend to be the most common, and for good reason. Too much time between meetings leads to loss of commitment, and human nature starts to take over (in other words, people get bored, lethargic, disinterested, jaded or all four). Too many meetings and the members of your group start to get overwhelmed, not so much by the amount of reading that is due, but with the worry, usually mistaken, that there is too much reading and they'll never get to it: the dishes need washing, tomorrow is another day, I'm having trouble finding my way through the author's opening gambit, etc., etc. Once a month is also a great option (say, the first Tuesday of every month), since it gives the members the time to read the books under discussion, it is not overly demanding on anyone's time, and it gives the group as a whole the regularity that helps everyone remember this shared commitment.

After your club has decided how often to meet, some thought should go into being adaptable to the seasons. Various holidays scattered throughout the year can throw your reading schedule out of kilter. Summer can be particularly disruptive. Your group may decide that summer is the perfect time to read one of the biggies, precisely because other pressures are not quite so plentiful: *Don Quixote* by Cervantes or *One Hundred Years of Solitude* by Gabriel García Márquez or Tolstoy's *Anna Karenina* or *Voltaire's Bastards* by John Ralston Saul. Or you may decide that the summer is the perfect time to meet only on one special occasion or possibly not to meet at all. Trying to get everyone there, with holidays, family visits and sundry other interruptions is sometimes more work than it's worth. For the summer, we suggest picking a substantial book, but allowing two or so months to read it. Let's be realistic and a little insistent here: how many more years can you really put off reading *War and Peace, Moby Dick* or some of the other monumental books you've always wanted to read?

How Many People Should Be in Your Group. Once again, common sense has a lot to say here. Too many members in your group and some people will get left in the conversational dust; too few and the conversation lacks perspective and fresh insights. As we've said earlier, as we write this book we envision a group with between eight and twelve members at each meeting (which would probably mean an original list of about fifteen), though we have seen very successful groups constituted of four close friends meeting over a cup of coffee, or of one hundred complete strangers crammed into an auditorium. Again, a great deal depends on your needs, your means (how many friends and acquaintances do you actually have, anyway? If your job is operating a lighthouse, your options may be limited!) and your intuition.

Don't forget that you can always add and subtract from your group as you go along. Some people will naturally fall by the wayside, for any number of good reasons, while others will hear about your group and want to join. Adaptability is once again the key here. We know of one group that has had the same eight members for years and another group that seems forever in a state of numerical flux. Both work, and work well.

Where Your Group Should Meet. We have both been involved with groups that have met in public places and others that have met in private homes. If it's to be a public place your group has to be able to isolate itself, to some degree, from the other people and the noise and the business around you. Our current group meets in a pub not far from work. We gather in an out-of-the-way corner on the third floor. It is relatively quiet and relatively removed from the action, but not so much so that we can't see the wait staff when the time comes to order the next round of beer or nachos. Although more costly than meeting at a person's house—where food and drinks are available at market cost—there are no dishes left for the poor sod who lives there and everyone feels equally at home (well, some of us feel more "at home" in the pub than others, but that's a whole other story).

If it's a private residence, your group must ensure that the preparation and cleaning is shared among all members, either by rotating the location or doling out the responsibilities in an equitable manner. Most successful clubs that meet at private residences do so on a rotating basis, so that no one person has to assume more responsibility than others. Your group, and especially the person in whose home you meet, must be able to shut out the outside world for the duration of the meeting. Ringing phones, inquisitive children or other family members, needy pets and other household activities (a TV blaring in the next room, "Mom, I know you're meeting right now but I need twenty dollars for the pizza delivery") can all scuttle a lively conversation quickly and can lead to stilted exchanges.

Your group must also ensure that the space is large enough, that there are enough chairs and that the surroundings, although they need not be grand, must at least be congenial. Meeting in a rec room in a damp basement with teenage posters plastering the walls can obviously influence the comfort level of your group members, at least initially. At the same time, meeting at the pub with friends you met in church may be equally ill conceived. Solicit the input of your club members when choosing a regular spot.

Even after you sort out these issues, there are some important considerations if your book club is to succeed. In particular we offer the following two bits of wisdom:

Make Sure People Read the Books. Every member of your group must be ready and willing to read the books that the group has selected. Nothing is more frustrating for members who have read the book than a few members who have not. This situation has lead to more than a few hard feelings and resentments, and of course to the demise of groups altogether. We have heard of groups that refuse to allow members to show up for a meeting if they haven't read the book, but that seems a bit harsh. We think that it is better to instil just the right amount of obligation with a dash of guilt than to ostracize and risk alienating an otherwise important member of your group.

Members must also be prepared to read the books well, not just flip through the pages. Woody Allen said that he once took a speed reading course and then read *Moby Dick* in eight minutes. His complete critical commentary on one of the monuments of world literature was: "It's all about whaling." We encourage, or rather you should encourage, all members of your book club to be a bit more dedicated with their reading and insightful with their commentary than Woody. (And if you find someone hiding *Cliff's Notes* under their jacket, then you've got real problems!)

Make Sure You Start on Time. You must also make sure that the meeting of your club starts on time. As one of our members asks, "how will the late comers know they were late if we don't start on time?" Knowing that the group will start without them is often a sure-fire way to get individual stragglers to arrive on time.

Decisions, Decisions (Part Two)

After your group has met a few times, it will begin to develop a life and a logic all its own. As a group, you will all soon realize what concerns are uppermost in members' minds and how to cope with or encourage them, what issues seem to drag the spirits of the group down, who are the members who never manage to finish the book, when to cut your losses and lurch on to the next book on your list, and a myriad of other qualities of your group. The basic navigational tools for developing a successful group are not so different from those used in developing a successful home life or work life. In brief, you've got to know when to express your opinion and when to keep quiet so that others can express their opinions. After that, the group will hopefully come into its own. The better you do your job prior to the first meeting, the less guidance the group needs once it is off the ground.

The mechanics of a healthy, self-sustaining book club that provides insight and pleasure for its members include the following decisions:

Should We Bring in Authors, Special Lecturers or Experts? There are groups that function best when they are a select and unchanging clutch of good friends who talk among themselves every meeting and have no desire for outside resources. But we have found that many groups benefit greatly from including guest authors, professors, critics or other specialists.

Bringing in an "outsider" does several things: it shakes up the group and focuses the attention of members and their conversations in new ways; it mixes up the dynamic of the group—some people known for their wise cracks or their quietness might very well surprise you when the book's author is present at the meeting; and, above all, it provides the group with fresh insights and information that could not be found elsewhere.

We suggest that you invite guests (either writers or lecturers) to your group at least once a year. Of course, trying to get Alice Munro or Thomas Pynchon to your group may not be practical, but there are many authors who are willing—for the price of a meal or a few beverages, or to ensure the sale of ten more copies of their book—to come and talk to your group. A member of your group might very well know someone who knows someone who knows a few authors. Or try contacting authors through their publishers or through resources found at your local library or bookstores. Asking your local college or university English department is another way to ferret them out. Many libraries and bookstores also invite writers to read from their works. Many well-known authors, while on tour promoting a book, have spoken to groups much smaller than your group. Take a chance. Many authors are thrilled just to be asked, especially if they don't have to travel too far to get there and the meeting is mostly informal. Most writers are more than happy for the attention to their work and to hear the comments of interested readers. There are poets, historians, writers of fiction, essayists, journalists and critics who will be only too happy to come to your book club. Take it from us, writers don't feel as though they get nearly enough attention in our society. They will probably jump at the chance.

If you're still feeling shy or at a loss as to how to invite a writer to come to your group, then bring your group to the writer. Arrange for your group to attend a local reading and then go off and discuss the writer's work and his or her public persona.

You may also want to think about bringing in non-experts, that is, friends or family. One group we heard of has a guest night every year at which each member is encouraged to bring one person. New members for the group have been found as a result of these meetings and the conversations always have a fresh twist.

Our book club recently asked novelist Paul Quarrington to come to one of our meetings to discuss his Governor General's Award–winning book *Whale Music*. (We were able to ask Quarrington to come because someone in our group knew his agent, and he was happy to oblige. However, even if we hadn't known the agent, we could have invited other authors by contacting their publishers or just by looking them up in the phone book.)

It was, without question, one of our most successful meetings. The tone was set immediately by Quarrington himself, who arrived with his book agent about a half-hour after we had all assembled. He was informal and engaging, witty and relaxed.

We met, as usual, at a local pub. Despite the background hum of glasses clinking and people in other rooms talking and generic music rumbling through the pub's speakers, we managed to have an informative and interesting conversation in which everyone participated.

The evening started with Quarrington reading a short passage from the book. The questions that we then asked ranged from soliciting his thoughts on producing a book that closely alluded to a living icon of rock and roll, Brian Wilson of the Beach Boys, to whether he writes on a computer or long-hand, to discussing his choice of individual words. One member was particularly interested in his use of the word "horripilated," to which Quarrington replied, tongue firmly in cheek: "Well, I use that word quite often in conversation."

Not all of the questions we asked were particularly insightful, nor were they well crafted. But in such a setting it really didn't matter. Like any seasoned writer and interviewee, Quarrington was gracious and informative with his answers. He also volunteered snippets of gossip about other writers and very forthright observations about his own work and ambitions. He noted that at one party he attended not long after he won the Governor General's Award another writer was lamenting the fact that Mordecai Richler had not won for *Solomon Gursky Was Here*, but instead a work by "some mediocrity." The "mediocrity" in question then went up to introduce himself to the embarrassed originator of the comment.

At the end of the meeting Quarrington signed all of our copies of the book. He even drew a picture in each of our copies: he changed the "Q" in his last name into a rather portly figure reminiscent of the character Des Howell in the book.

The only cost sustained by the club that evening was the Guinness for Quarrington and the beer for his agent. A humble expense compared to the great pleasure and insight we all had.

Should We See the Film of the Book and Read Magazine Articles, Reviews or Other Secondary Material? We have found that secondary resources often provide a valuable spark to book discussions. There are many films that cannot begin to cope with the depth and passion and imagination built into the book itself, into the richness and depth of the written word, but there are films that do manage to do justice to the book. Some films are faithful to the book while others freely move far from the intents of the original. Among the most successful are the following book-related movies:

* *The Dead*, from the James Joyce short story.
* *Death in Venice*, from the novella by Thomas Mann.
* *The World According to Garp*, from the John Irving novel.
* *Whale Music*, from the Paul Quarrington novel.
* *The Handmaid's Tale*, from the Margaret Atwood novel.
* *The English Patient*, from the Michael Ondaatje novel.
* *The Apprenticeship of Duddy Kravitz*, from the Mordecai Richler novel.
* *The Age of Innocence*, from the Edith Wharton novel.
* *Sense and Sensibility* and *Emma*, from the Jane Austen classics.
* *Beloved*, from the Toni Morrison novel.
* Numerous Shakespeare adaptations, particularly those by Kenneth Branagh and Laurence Olivier.

You may also want to try *Naked Lunch, Margaret's Museum, The Razor's Edge* (the Tyrone Power version, not the Bill Murray version), *To Kill a Mockingbird, A Passage to India* (or almost any film made from an E. M. Forster novel) or *A Clockwork Orange*.

If your group chooses to use a film to enliven your conversation about a novel, be very careful in your selections, since many a bad film has been made from a great novel (many an American Literature class has been spoiled by the professor encouraging the class to see Demi Moore's *The Scarlet Letter*).

Other material such as book reviews, critical articles, interviews with the author, even entries from literary guidebooks or encyclopedia can be very helpful in fleshing out authors and their work. It might be best to delegate one person per meeting to do the research, rather than several people all showing up at the meeting with the same articles. With the Internet, it is now not necessary to be living on a university campus or have doctoral-level research capabilities. Information is readily available on many authors through various search engines, but don't forget your local library. Reviews of, articles on and interviews with, for example, Carol Shields, are accessible at most libraries. Ask your local librarian for help searching through newspapers, magazines and journals for relevant information.

Another way to liven up your book club is to listen to recordings of the item you're reading. One of the very first recordings ever made was Alfred, Lord Tennyson, reading his poetry. Unfortunately, the wax cylinders on which the recording was made were left near a hot water pipe and now only eight lines of a recorded poem remain. But Tennyson's booming monotone voice lends them a powerful force. Richard Burton reading Dylan Thomas's poems or the dramatic readings on CBC Radio of Michael Ondaatje's *The English Patient* or Margaret Laurence's *The Stone Angel*, for example, are equally fascinating and insightful. Much writing is meant to be read out loud (our literature did, after all, evolve out of an oral tradition), as though it were an oral poem or story. In the hands and on the lips of a gifted storyteller, the best literature truly comes alive, and reading aloud may help group members gain added insight and inspiration.

What About Special Book-Related Outings for Your Group? Organized talks, lectures and readings are also great ways for your group to get closer to writers of both fiction and non-fiction. Many libraries, bookstores, universities and colleges bring in writers throughout the year. In larger cities the resources are obviously more plentiful, but even smaller towns sometimes have writers in residence at local libraries or colleges. Search them out. Most writers are more than happy to know that people are actually reading their books and talking about the issues they had in mind while writing them. If your local bookstore does not have a writers' series, encourage it to organize one or help to organize one by offering your time, a guaranteed audience and the promise of book sales (if you have a book club, you have consumer power, and if you have consumer power, you might as well use it to the benefit of your club).

What About Other Outings for Your Group? There is no reason why you have to limit your book group's activities to books. We know of a group that took a bicycle tour of the wine region around Niagara Falls and another that went overnight camping near the West Coast Trail on Vancouver Island. In both cases the groups came back invigorated and with new insights into their fellow members. "We had a great time," said one of the wine tour participants. "The group loosened up considerably the more wineries we visited and although we didn't make an effort to avoid all discussions of books, we did find ourselves talking more about the books than we thought we would. We were reading a Mordecai Richler book at the time, *Joshua Then and Now*. There's drinking in that book, you know!...We were able to rationalize our trip by saying that Richler would have approved."

Your group may also have a member who has a cottage or someone who knows of a secluded beach or park where you can all gather for a picnic or a swim. Even a special outing at a local upscale restaurant can be a treat for the group, and can help draw the members closer together. From time to time, every person or group needs a break from the predictable. There's no reason to treat your book club any differently.

Should You Alternate Your Reading? Your group need not be wedded to either fiction or memoirs or history. If you find your meetings starting to flag, toss in an assignment that is a bit unexpected. One of the most successful meetings of our club was when one of our members photocopied Martin Luther King, Jr.'s "Letter from Birmingham City Jail" for us to all read and be ready to discuss at our next meeting. Our subsequent discussion ranged widely over issues of racism, television stereotypes, education, the state's inability to confront individual pockets of ignorance, and a host of other issues. That King's eloquent letter was written in the margins of a newspaper in his cell, and that he would be dead five months later, added to our impassioned discussion.

Every once in a while we also throw in a poetry night, where each member reads aloud a favourite poem, which we then briefly discuss. The poets selected have ranged from Walt Whitman to W. B. Yeats, and the discussions have mostly been both entertaining and discerning. One of the pleasures of bringing poetry to a meeting is that it is usually read out loud. One of our members has memorized quite a few poems and to hear him recite them from memory is transfixing.

Should You Duplicate Your Reading? Why not try reading the same book twice, say a year or two apart? You'll be amazed at the different insights and sensibilities you bring to the same book. Nancy Mitford once said, "I have only ever read one book in my life, and that is *White Fang*. It's so frightfully good I've never bothered to read another." We know of a group in New York City that reads only *Finnegans Wake*, James Joyce's final masterwork, one brief passage at a time. Reading only one book might be rather extreme for your group, but you'll be surprised at the new things you see in a book the second time around. Your group may want to take a few cracks at an Alice Munro short story or *Under the Volcano* by Malcolm Lowry. You will probably find that reading a book multiple times at different points in your life is a good habit to get into.

How Do We Get the Discussion Started? Despite the desire to keep your group on track, there will be times when your club has trouble even getting moving. You will probably find that there will be times when everyone seems half-asleep or would rather talk about TV than about books. Here are some ideas to get the talk moving:

∗ Suggest everyone write down the most disturbing or passionate or joyful scene in the book: you'll be surprised at the breadth of answers.

∗ Choose one of the secondary characters and discuss why this person is important to the structure and development of the book.

∗ Pick out the most curious word of the book or the word that irritates you the most; words are the foundation of all this discussion and your group should be able to sustain a discussion of some duration about the author's use of one or a few words.

∗ Talk theme: what is it that the author is trying to say?

∗ Look at symbols: every word, every image, is a symbol of something or for something else; don't fall into the trap of sentimentality or silliness, but talk about what specific images or phrases represent.

∗ Try comparative reading: how does this book relate, or not relate, to other books you've been reading?

For a much more extensive discussion of possible topics, or to see how these discussion topics can be played out over the course of a meeting on a particular book, read our special sample readings in the following chapters on F. Scott Fitzgerald's *The Great Gatsby* and Susanna Moodie's *Roughing It in the Bush*.

If your group really is not able to gel on a given night, don't worry about it. Even the most industrious and devoted groups hit an off night from time to time. Don't sweat it. In these situations it probably is better to order a few more glasses of wine or talk about movies or play a game of pool or go for a walk or any other non-bookish thing that strikes your fancy. Why push the point if the energy is just not there? You will only alienate club members instead of showing them that the club is flexible enough to accommodate any mood.

The Only Thing Permanent Is Change

The main thing to remember about your book club is that it is forever in the process of change and adaptation. Forming and sustaining a book club is a fluid process and there is no sense in resisting the inevitable. Keep the club organized within a few gentle parameters and let it move at its own speed and in its own direction. What you'll have in the end is a club where all members have some sense of ownership, and discussions that really start to sing.

The aim should be to enliven the imagination and get your members engaged in the text in front of them. There will be moments when the discussion hums along and everyone participates and has a great time. It won't happen all the time, but it will happen. Enjoy it when it occurs.

All That Jazz:

Sample Fiction Reading and Discussion

Everyone recognizes me in my book,
and my book in me.

MONTAIGNE

BYOB (Bring Your Own Book)

After all the thinking, wondering, pondering, questioning and otherwise driving yourself crazy about how best to start your book club, what it ultimately comes down to is you and a group of friends, colleagues or neighbours sitting in a loosely formed circle, books in hands, puzzling over what to say, how to begin, where to go from here. So how do you begin? How do people effectively talk about books in such a way that everyone present can benefit from the experience? This is what *Build a Better Book Club* is really all about, because this is what is going to make, sustain or break your book club.

Every group will want to discuss different subjects and adopt different approaches to discussing books. No two groups are the same, though some will be more intense, erudite, informed, constructive and ultimately more rewarding than others. These are the conversations that we are trying to help you promote. For this reason, we have chosen *The Great Gatsby* by the American novelist F. Scott Fitzgerald as our sample fiction reading, since it is widely read, taught and praised. Or, as critic Tony Tanner writes, it is "the most perfectly crafted work of fiction to have come out of America." It is also one of the juiciest books ever written; your book club could make worse selections!

You should remember, however, that this is just one sample reading of one book to give you some good ideas on how to begin your own discussions. There are of course a multitude of other directions, topics and conclusions that your group might address. But by offering our sample reading, we hope that we can provide some seeds from which your own discussions can grow and flourish.

"Now I Know My A-B-Cs"— How to Read

To a great extent, the topics of conversation in a book club meeting depend upon a variety of different factors: the nature of the book, the members of the club, the quantity of Guinness or sherry flowing. These factors also inform the order in which topics will be discussed.

However, there are a number of topics, listed below, that your club can use as a guideline for any discussion, and that inform our reading of excerpts from *The Great Gatsby* and from *Roughing It in the Bush* discussed in the next chapter. For every discussion, you may want to begin with the basic scaffolding on which all writing is built: the events of the author's life, the historical context, the genre of the work. Where your conversations go from there, in terms of more analytical topics, is up to you.

The following is a list of critical approaches to reading to help get you started. There are many more complete reference guides and dictionaries of literary terms available that you may also choose to consult.

Author Biography. The basic, available information on the events of an author's life that may have some bearing on his or her work, including place and year of birth, places where the author has lived, social class, family and social influences, education, artistic influences, other works by the same author and on the author.

Character. The role of all primary and secondary characters in driving the story forward. All characters have a purpose in any work of writing. Often the author expresses his or her own views and opinions through the voices of the characters, or characters are used to express opposite points of view. Readers may choose to discuss the characters' morality, insight or lack of insight into occurrences around them, religious beliefs, politics, artistic temperament and a multitude of other possibilities.

Historical Context and Setting. There are two complementary approaches to this topic: the time frame in which the author wrote the book and the time frame that the author is writing about—not always the same thing. An author cannot help but be informed in some way by the political, religious, aesthetic and cultural period in which he or she lived. Authors often either celebrate the beliefs of their society, or challenge them, or, as with someone like James Joyce or Jane Austen, do both at the same time. When authors write about eras other than their own, your group may wish to investigate how each author characterizes that other period.

Imagery and Symbolism. A dictionary will tell you that a symbol is any action, phrase or thing that represents something else. Often a symbol or an image in a work represents an aspect of the author's or character's internal state. Symbols can also be used to represent large historical, political, religious or cultural events. A fire in one book might represent a character's passion, while in another book it might represent corruption and decline on a grand scale. Because symbols are by definition slippery and subject to interpretation, addressing the symbols in the book you're reading can lead to the best and most complex discussions.

Other Sources. We live in a rich age where books are made into movies, movies are made into books, and armies of academics earn a living writing about any book ever published. Some of the sources that you may want to investigate include reviews written at the time the book was published, more recent academic discussions of the work, biographies of the author, movies made from the work and other works by the same author that have some bearing. In some books, authors may refer to music, books, food that you may wish to listen to, read, eat as a way of gaining insight into the work. Even the grandchildren of F. Scott Fitzgerald have recently asked for a brand of Fitzgerald furniture to be designed. Your group can discuss Gatsby while kicking your feet up onto a Nick Carraway Ottoman.

Role and Voice of the Narrator. The narrator or voice of the book you are reading—whether the piece is an autobiography, a poem or a work of fiction—can be either believable or dishonest, can be ironic or mathematically precise in its presentation of the facts, can be all-knowing or only aware of a small sliver of the world. As you read any book, pay close attention not only to what is being said, but also to who is saying it and how it is said. The narrator of a work can be the author, or someone or something else chosen by the author to tell the events of the tale. You should also decide if you want to believe what you are being told or if you should treat the information with a pinch of salt. Be aware that sometimes the narrator's role is to mislead the reader.

Style. The style of a work is how it is presented. The language can be journalistic and straightforward, poetic and allusive, or anything in between. How an author writes—short, snappy sentences à la Ernest Hemingway, in a regional tone like Alice Walker, or poetic and lush as in Ondaatje's *The English Patient*—has a great effect on how you read and absorb the story being told. The style of a work often reflects the characters, themes and general context of a text.

Theme. Perhaps the easiest way for your club to delve into the serious issues of a book is to determine and debate the themes of the work. This is, after all, the way in which we were taught to read and analyze books way back in grade school or early high school. Each of us can remember our Grade 7 or 8 teacher telling us that the theme of a book is the message or the moral or the lesson that the author was trying to teach us. Usually we were reading something like *The Lord of the Flies* and the author, we were inevitably told, was teaching us something about "man's inhumanity to man." (Apparently gender-neutral language hadn't yet crept into the school system.) Our English teachers way back then were Mrs. Solomon and Sister Dickinson. Well, Mrs. Solomon and Sister Dickinson, we're here to tell you that you weren't that far off the mark.

It may be a little too simplistic to say that the theme of a book is the lesson that the author is teaching us, but that definition at least gestures in the right direction. A more accurate description might be that a theme could be any of the general issues of our lives that the book touches or sheds light upon. For example, if a book deals with men and women in particularly punishing relationships, then the members of the group would not be wrong to suggest that the ways in which men and women treat each other is an important theme of the book. If the book under discussion is a fictional or non-fictional examination of a large multinational corporation's irresponsible actions in polluting a river, then the group can rightly suggest that the author is concerned, in a more general way, with the way we are destroying the planet, and can begin a discussion on that subject both as it relates specifically to the work in question and in a more general sense.

Addressing the themes of a book is a very constructive way to develop your discussion of a particular work, and it is also a good way to allow the conversation to move effortlessly into a more general dialogue, where members can offer broader insights and opinions on topics related to the book club. Some of the best debates begin this way. For instance, if your club is discussing a novel in which one of the characters offers some brutally racist opinions, one of the members might be inclined to suggest that these ideas are typical of most people in our society. A second member might strongly disagree, saying that while there are certainly instances of racism in our society, those who share such intolerant feelings are in the minority. A third member may suggest that racism is more prevalent in certain sectors of society than in others, and it therefore may not be as obvious among this group as it would be among another. The first participant might then offer Nazi Germany as an example of an entire society where latent racist feelings suddenly surfaced in the majority. By this point, the book has sparked a debate in which every member of the group is clamouring to have a say. And this, after all, is the ultimate goal: talk leading to insight and a better informed view of the topic at hand.

Let's Get Down to It

What follows is an excerpt from *The Great Gatsby* by F. Scott Fitzgerald. We then take you through a sample book club discussion and reading of the work (and of *Roughing It in the Bush* in the next chapter), using some or all of the above discussion topics in an order appropriate to the excerpt and the work in general.

THE GREAT GATSBY BY F. SCOTT FITZGERALD:

Excerpts from Chapter III

There was music from my neighbour's house through the summer nights. In his blue gardens men and girls came and went like moths among the whisperings and the champagne and the stars. At high tide in the afternoon I watched his guests diving from the tower of his raft or taking the sun on the hot sand of his beach while his two motor boats slit the waters of the Sound, drawing aquaplanes over cataracts of foam. On week-ends his Rolls-Royce became an omnibus, bearing parties to and from the city, between nine in the morning and long past midnight, while his station wagon scampered like a brisk yellow bug to meet all trains. And on Mondays eight servants, including an extra gardener, toiled all day with mops and scrubbing-brushes and hammers and garden-shears, repairing the ravages of the night before.

Every Friday five crates of oranges and lemons arrived from a fruiterer in New York—every Monday these same oranges and lemons left his back door in a pyramid of pulpless halves. There was a machine in the kitchen which could extract the juice of two hundred oranges in half an hour if a little button was pressed two hundred times by a butler's thumb.

At least once a fortnight a corps of caterers came down with several hundred feet of canvas and enough coloured lights to make a Christmas tree of Gatsby's enormous garden. On buffet tables, garnished with glistening hors-d'oeuvre, spiced baked hams crowded against salads of harlequin designs and pastry pigs and turkeys bewitched to a dark gold. In the main hall a bar with a real brass rail was set up, and stocked with gins and liquors and with cordials so long forgotten that most of his female guests were too young to know one from another.

By seven o'clock the orchestra has arrived, no thin five-piece affair, but a whole pitful of oboes and trombones and saxophones and viols and cornets and piccolos, and low and high drums. The last swimmers have come in from the beach now and are dressing upstairs; the cars from New York are parked five deep in the drive, and already the halls and salons and verandas are gaudy with primary colours, and hair bobbed in strange new ways, and shawls beyond the dreams of Castile. The bar is in full swing, and floating rounds of cocktails permeate the garden outside, until the air is alive with chatter and laughter, and casual innuendo and introductions forgotten on the spot, and enthusiastic meetings between women who never knew each other's names.

The lights grow brighter as the earth lurches away from the sun, and now the orchestra is playing yellow cocktail music, and the opera of voices pitches a key higher. Laughter is easier minute by minute, spilled with prodigality, tipped out at a cheerful word. The groups change more swiftly, swell with new arrivals, dissolve and form in the same breath; already there are wanderers, confident girls who weave here and there among the stouter and more stable, become for a sharp, joyous moment the center of a group, and then, excited with triumph, glide on through the sea-change of faces and voices and colour under the constantly changing light.

Suddenly one of these gypsies, in trembling opal, seizes a cocktail out of the air, dumps it down for courage and, moving her hands like Frisco, dances out alone on the canvas platform. A momentary hush; the orchestra leader varies his rhythm obligingly for her, and there is a burst of chatter as the erroneous news goes around that she is Gilda Gray's understudy from the Follies. The party has begun.

I believe that on the first night I went to Gatsby's house I was one of the few guests who had actually been invited. People were not invited—they went there. They got into automobiles which bore them out to Long Island, and somehow they ended up at Gatsby's door. Once there they were introduced by somebody who knew Gatsby, and after that they conducted themselves according to the rules of behavior associated with an amusement park. Sometimes they came and went without having met Gatsby at all, came for the party with a simplicity of heart that was its own ticket of admission.

I had been actually invited. A chauffeur in a uniform of robin's-egg blue crossed my lawn early that Saturday morning with a surprisingly formal note from his employer: the honour would be entirely Gatsby's, it said, if I would attend his "little party" that night. He had seen me several times, and had intended to call on me long before, but a peculiar combination of circumstances had prevented it—signed Jay Gatsby, in a majestic hand.

Dressed up in white flannels I went over to his lawn a little after seven, and wandered around rather ill at ease among swirls and eddies of people I didn't know—though here and there was a face I had noticed on the commuting train. I was immediately struck by the number of young Englishmen dotted about; all well dressed, all looking a little hungry, and all talking in low, earnest voices to solid and prosperous Americans. I was sure that they were all selling something: bonds or insurance or automobiles. They were at least agonizingly aware of the easy money in the vicinity and convinced that it was theirs for a few words in the right key.

As soon as I arrived I made an attempt to find my host, but the two or three people of whom I asked his whereabouts stared at me in such an amazed way, and denied so vehemently any knowledge of his movements, that I slunk off in the direction of the cocktail table—the only place in the garden where a single man could linger without looking purposeless and alone.

~

The bar, where we glanced first, was crowded, but Gatsby was not there. She [Jordan Baker] couldn't find him from the top of the steps, and he wasn't on the veranda. On a chance we tried an important-looking door, and walked into a high Gothic library, panelled with carved English Oak, and probably transported complete from some ruin overseas.

A stout, middle-aged man, with enormous owl-eyed spectacles was sitting somewhat drunk on the edge of a great table, staring with unsteady concentration at the shelves of books. As we entered he wheeled excitedly around and examined Jordan from head to foot.

"What do you think?" he demanded impetuously.

"About what?"

He waved his hand toward the book-shelves.

"About that. As a matter of fact you needn't bother to ascertain. I ascertained. They're real."

"The books?"

He nodded.

"Absolutely real—have pages and everything. I thought they'd be a nice durable cardboard. Matter of fact, they're absolutely real. Pages and—Here! Lemme show you."

Taking our skepticism for granted, he rushed to the bookcases and returned with Volume One of the "Stoddard Lectures."

"See!" he cried triumphantly. "It's a bona-fide piece of printed matter. It fooled me. This fella's a regular Belasco. It's a triumph. What thoroughness! What realism! Knew when to stop too—didn't cut the pages. But what do you want? What do you expect?"

He snatched the book from me and replaced it hastily on its shelf muttering that if one brick was removed the whole library was liable to collapse.

"Who brought you?" he demanded. "Or did you just come? I was brought. Most people were brought."

Jordan looked at him alertly, cheerfully without answering.

"I was brought by a woman named Roosevelt," he continued. "Mrs Claud Roosevelt. Do you know her? I met her somewhere last night. I've been drunk for about a week now, and I thought it might sober me up to sit in a library."

"Has it?"

"A little bit, I think. I can't tell yet. I've only been here an hour. Did I tell you about the books? They're real. They're —"

"You told us."

We shook hands with him gravely and went back outdoors.

There was dancing now on the canvas in the garden; old men pushing young girls backward in eternal graceless circles, superior couples holding each other tortuously, fashionably and keeping in the corners—and a great number of single girls dancing individualistically or relieving the orchestra for a moment of the burden of the banjo or the traps. By midnight the hilarity had increased. A celebrated tenor had sung in Italian, and a notorious contralto had sung in jazz, and between the numbers people were doing "stunts" all over the garden, while happy, vacuous bursts of laughter rose toward the summer sky. A pair of stage twins—who turned out to be the girls in yellow—did a baby act in costume, and champagne was served in glasses bigger than finger-bowls. The moon had risen higher, and floating in the Sound was a triangle of silver scales, trembling a little to the stiff, tinny drip of the banjoes on the lawn.

I was still with Jordan Baker. We were sitting at a table with a man of about my age and a rowdy little girl, who gave way upon the slightest provocation to uncontrollable laughter. I was enjoying myself now. I had taken two finger-bowls of champagne, and the scene had changed before my eyes into something significant, elemental, and profound.

At a lull in the entertainment the man looked at me and smiled.

"Your face is familiar," he said politely. "Weren't you in the First Division during the war?"

"Why, yes. I was in the Twenty-eighth Infantry."

"I was in the Seventh Infantry until June nineteen-eighteen. I knew I'd seen you somewhere before."

We talked for a moment about some wet, grey little villages in France. Evidently he lived in this vicinity, for he told me that he had just bought a hydroplane, and was going to try it out in the morning.

"Want to go with me, old sport? Just near the shore along the Sound."

"What time?"

"Any time that suits you best."

It was on the tip of my tongue to ask his name when Jordan looked around and smiled.

"Having a gay time now?" she inquired.

"Much better." I turned again to my new acquaintance. "This is an unusual party for me. I haven't even seen the host. I live over there—" I waved my hand at the invisible hedge in the distance, "and this man Gatsby sent over his chauffeur with an invitation."

For a moment he looked at me as if he failed to understand.

"I'm Gatsby," he said suddenly.

"What!" I exclaimed. "Oh, I beg your pardon."

"I thought you knew, old sport. I'm afraid I'm not a very good host."

He smiled understandingly—much more than understandingly. It was one of those rare smiles with a quality of eternal reassurance in it, that you may come across four or five times in life. It faced—or seemed to face—the whole eternal world for an instant, and then concentrated on *you* with an irresistible prejudice in your favor. It understood you just so far as you wanted to be understood, believed in you as you would like to believe in yourself, and assured you that it had precisely the impression of you that, at your best, you hoped to convey. Precisely at that point it vanished—and I was looking at an elegant young rough-neck, a year or two over thirty, whose elaborate formality of speech just missed being absurd. Some time before he introduced himself I'd got a strong impression that he was picking his words with care.

Almost at the moment when Mr Gatsby identified himself a butler hurried toward him with the information that Chicago was calling him on the wire. He excused himself with a small bow that included each of us in turn.

"If you want anything just ask for it, old sport," he urged me. "Excuse me. I will rejoin you later."

When he was gone I turned immediately to Jordan—constrained to assure her of my surprise. I had expected that Mr Gatsby would be a florid and corpulent person in his middle years.

"Who is he?" I demanded. "Do you know?"

"He's just a man named Gatsby."

"Where is he from, I mean? And what does he do?"

"Now *you*'re started on the subject," she answered with a wan smile. "Well, he told me once he was an Oxford man."

A dim background started to take shape behind him, but at her next remark it faded away.

"However, I don't believe it."

"Why not?"

"I don't know," she insisted, "I just don't think he went there."

Something in her tone reminded me of the other girl's "I think he killed a man," and had the effect of stimulating my curiosity. I would have accepted without question the information that Gatsby sprang from the swamps of Louisiana or from the lower East Side of New York. That was comprehensible. But young men didn't—at least in my provincial inexperience I believed they didn't—drift coolly out of nowhere and buy a palace on Long Island Sound.

"Anyhow, he gives large parties," said Jordan, changing the subject with an urban distaste for the concrete. "And I like large parties. They're so intimate. At small parties there isn't any privacy."

The large room was full of people. One of the girls in yellow was playing the piano, and beside her stood a tall, red-haired young lady from a famous chorus, engaged in song. She had drunk a quantity of champagne, and during the course of her song she had decided, ineptly, that everything was very very sad—she was not only singing, she was weeping too. Whenever there was a pause in the song she filled it with gasping, broken sobs, and then took up the lyric again in a quavering soprano. The tears coursed down her cheeks— not freely, however, for when they came into contact with her heavily beaded eyelashes they assumed an inky colour, and pursued the rest of their way in slow black rivulets. A humorous suggestion was made that she sing the notes on her face, whereupon she threw up her hands, sank into a chair, and went off into a deep vinous sleep.

"She had a fight with a man who says he's her husband," explained a girl at my elbow.

I looked around. Most of the remaining women were now having fights with men said to be their husbands. Even Jordan's party, the quartet from East Egg, were rent asunder by dissension. One of the men was talking with curious intensity to a young actress, and his wife, after attempting to laugh at the situation in a dignified and indifferent way, broke down entirely and resorted to flank attacks—at intervals she appeared suddenly at his side like an angry diamond and hissed: "You promised!" into his ear.

The reluctance to go home was not confined to wayward men. The hall was at present occupied by two deplorably sober men and their highly indignant wives. The wives were sympathizing with each other in slightly raised voices.

"Whenever he sees I'm having a good time he wants to go home."

"Never heard anything so selfish in my life."

"We're always the first ones to leave."

"So are we."

"Well, we're almost the last tonight," said one of the men sheepishly. "The orchestra left half an hour ago."

In spite of the wives' agreement that such malevolence was beyond credibility, the dispute ended in a short struggle and both wives were lifted, kicking, into the night.

As I waited for my hat in the hall the door of the library opened and Jordan Baker and Gatsby came out together. He was saying some last word to her but the eagerness in his manner tightened abruptly into formality as several people approached him to say good-bye.

Jordan's party were calling impatiently to her from the porch but she lingered for a moment to shake hands.

"I've just heard the most amazing thing," she whispered. "How long were we in there?"

"Why, about an hour."

"It was—simply amazing," she repeated abstractedly. "But I swore I wouldn't tell it and here I am tantalizing you." She yawned gracefully in my face. "Please come and see me....Phone book....Under the name of Mrs Sigourney Howard....My aunt...." She was hurrying off as she talked—her brown hand waved a jaunty salute as she melted into her party at the door.

Rather ashamed that on my first appearance I had stayed so late, I joined the last of Gatsby's guests, who were clustered around him. I wanted to explain that I'd hunted for him early in the evening and to apologize for not having known him in the garden.

"Don't mention it," he enjoined me eagerly. "Don't give it another thought, old sport." The familiar expression held no more familiarity than the hand which reassuringly brushed my shoulder. "And don't forget we're going up in the hydroplane tomorrow morning, at nine o'clock."

Then the butler, behind his shoulder:

"Philadelphia wants you on the phone, sir."

"All right, in a minute. Tell them I'll be right there....Good night."

"Good night."

"Good night." He smiled—and suddenly there seemed to be a pleasant significance in having been among the last to go, as if he had desired it all the time. "Good night, old sport....Good night."

⸺

Reading over what I have written so far, I see I have given the impression that the events of three nights several weeks apart were all that absorbed me. On the contrary, they were merely casual events in a crowded summer, and, until much later, they absorbed me infinitely less than my personal affairs.

Most of the time I worked. In the early morning the sun threw my shadow westward as I hurried down the white chasms of lower New York to the Probity Trust. I knew the other clerks and young bond-salesmen by their first names, and lunched with them in dark, crowded restaurants on little pig sausages and mashed potatoes and coffee. I even had a short affair with a girl who lived in Jersey City and worked in the accounting department, but her brother began throwing mean looks in my direction, so when she went on her vacation in July I let it blow quietly away.

—

Jordan Baker instinctively avoided clever, shrewd men, and now I saw that this was because she felt safer on a plane where any divergence from a code would be thought impossible. She was incurably dishonest. She wasn't able to endure being at a disadvantage and, given this unwillingness, I suppose she had begun dealing in subterfuges when she was very young in order to keep that cool, insolent smile turned to the world and yet satisfy the demands of her hard, jaunty body.

It made no difference to me. Dishonesty in a woman is a thing you never blame deeply—I was casually sorry, and then I forgot. It was on that same house-party that we had a curious conversation about driving a car. It started because she passed so close to some workmen that our fender flicked a button on one man's coat.

"You're a rotten driver," I protested. "Either you ought to be more careful, or you oughtn't to drive at all."

"I am careful."

"No, you're not."

"Well, other people are," she said lightly.

"What's that got to do with it?"

"They'll keep out of my way," she insisted. "It takes two to make an accident."

"Suppose you met somebody just as careless as yourself."

"I hope I never will," she answered. "I hate careless people. That's why I like you."

Her grey sun-strained eyes stared straight ahead, but she had deliberately shifted our relations, and for a moment I thought I loved her. But I am slow-thinking and full of interior rules that act as brakes on my desires, and I knew that first I had to get myself definitely out of that tangle back home. I'd been writing letters once a week and signing them: "Love, Nick," and all I could think of was how, when that certain girl played tennis, a faint mustache of perspiration appeared on her upper lip. Nevertheless there was a vague understanding that had to be tactfully broken off before I was free.

Every one suspects himself of at least one of the cardinal virtues, and this is mine: I am one of the few honest people that I have ever known.

Excerpted from The Great Gatsby *by F. Scott Fitzgerald, published by Scribner Classics in 1992.*

Reading *Gatsby*: "Hey Look at Mikey. He Likes It!"

Every book club discussion begins exactly the same way. Members of the group look at each other a little sheepishly, squirm a bit in their seats, look toward the ground or the ceiling as though inspiration is somehow etched into the concrete or the plaster or the shag carpeting. Then someone says those magical, time-honoured words that begin one of the least meaningful conversations in human history: "I liked it."

From here, the conversation will take on a life of its own, if for no other reason than in every group, reading every book, there will be those who "like it" and those who "don't like it." What is implied in this exchange? This phrase, by definition, means something different for every person. In the case of *The Great Gatsby*, for one person it will mean that she happened to visit Long Island with her parents long ago and she therefore feels that she has some kind of privileged perspective over the other group members in understanding the subtleties of the book. Somebody else in the group might consider himself an expert in American literature because he took a high school course decades ago, and an even greater judge of literary standards, and might feel commanding enough to make sweeping judgements about the influence of jazz on the syntax of the book, or how sight and blindness are the only themes of the book worth discussing.

Those in the group who didn't like the book are often simply saying that they felt bored while reading, or that they couldn't identify with the characters, use of language or situations, or that they just couldn't understand what the author was getting at. Some people, like our friend Howard, simply don't like fiction, feeling that they would prefer to remain in the "real" world rather than entering the imagination of someone they will never meet.

Inevitable as it might be, the I like it/I don't like it critical exchange is ultimately a conversational cul de sac. Although you can go on briefly to explain your reaction, there is no entry into a wider, richer understanding of the textual, thematic, intellectual intricacies of the book. As we will now show you, there are an almost infinite number of other ways to launch yourself into a challenging, insightful discussion of the book that you all have in your lap.

Author, Author: Biography and Related Information

Often the best place to begin any discussion of a book is to assign one person in the group (hopefully someone who has volunteered for the task) to research and present a brief biographical sketch on the author. This information is often easy to obtain. However, the more contemporary or obscure the author, the more difficult this task becomes. Think twice about volunteering in the case of researching Marvin Finklebarb's opus, *The Wives of the Brothers-in-Law Karamazov*, set to be published next week— see, we told you it was obscure!

Usually, the volunteer can obtain information from any number of sources, including the Internet (always the easiest, although sometimes not the most accurate or discerning), or the reference section at your local public library, where you can access encyclopedia, critical biographies of the author and introductions to other works by the same author. You may even be tempted to call the author directly, especially if someone in your group happens to know him or her. We suggest, however, that you try to avoid doing so, particularly in the middle of the night, especially if your book club happens to be discussing *Build a Better Book Club* or something by Charles Dickens.

Here is a sample biographical and bibliographical sketch that a book club might very easily find for F. Scott Fitzgerald:

Fitzgerald was born September 24, 1896, in St. Paul, Minnesota, and died December 21, 1940, in Hollywood, California. He attended Princeton University, but left in 1917 because of poor academic standing. He entered the U.S. Army in 1917, and in 1918 he met Zelda Sayre, the daughter of a Supreme Court judge from Alabama, whom he married in 1920 and with whom he endured a tempestuous relationship. In 1924 they moved to France, where they lived among such noteworthy expatriate authors as Ernest Hemingway, Morley Callaghan and Gertrude Stein. It was during these years that Fitzgerald and his contemporaries became known as the voices of a new Jazz Age generation of the 1920s. He was renowned for excessive drinking and mental instability. He became a scriptwriter in Hollywood in 1937.

His most important works include *This Side of Paradise*, his first book, published in 1920. It was considered a somewhat shocking exposé of the morality of youth in the early Jazz Age. The protagonist of the novel, Amory Blaine, attended Princeton and becomes involved in various literary activities and failed romances. His next book was a collection of short stories, *Tales of the Jazz Age*, published in 1922. Its publication was timed to coincide with the release of his novel *The Beautiful and the Damned*, which documents a dashing young couple who remain uninspired and unproductive as they wait for an inheritance, and eventually deteriorate into an alcoholic haze.

After publishing *The Great Gatsby* in 1925, Fitzgerald published a collection of short stories entitled *All the Sad Young Men* in 1926. *The Great Gatsby*, interestingly enough, had two other working titles: *Trimalchio in West Egg* and *Under the Red, White and Blue*. In 1934, his last completed novel, *Tender Is the Night*, appeared. It is a story of a psychiatrist who disintegrates after marrying one of his patients. His last novel, which he never completed, was titled *The Last Tycoon*, which chronicled the life of a Hollywood producer, Monroe Stahr, widely believed to be modelled upon the legendary film producer Irving Thalberg. Fitzgerald also wrote a book of essays entitled *The Crack-Up: With Other Uncollected Pieces, Note-Books, and Unpublished Letters* (1945). The essays are autobiographical and chronicle Fitzgerald's own deterioration late in his life.

Even from such limited snippets of information, your book club can get started on a worthwhile conversation about the relationship between the author and the book that you have all recently completed. The logical question to ask in a book club discussion would be: How can these facts give us further insight into Fitzgerald's work? From here, a member of your club might suggest that his failed academic pursuits suggest a relationship with the characters of *The Great Gatsby*, many of whom are identified by the colleges they attended, not the least of whom is Jay Gatsby and the question of whether or not he actually attended Oxford (or "Oggsford," as Mr. Wolfshiem calls it in Chapter IV of the novel). Nick Carraway also makes a point of mentioning that he graduated from New Haven (i.e., Yale University) within the opening two pages of the novel. Clearly your book club members will note the biographical relevance of this one seemingly minor point: Fitzgerald was obviously concerned with issues of one's educational past as a passport into some kind of wealthy, privileged or enlightened society. As Carraway says in the excerpt above, feigning coyness about his own education: "But young men didn't—at least in my provincial inexperience I believe they didn't—drift coolly out of nowhere and buy a palace on Long Island Sound."

Other questions begin to suggest themselves. For example, you may ask about Fitzgerald's personal relationships and their relevance to his work. From the fact that Fitzgerald endured a stormy relationship with his wife, Zelda, we see a definite cynicism in *The Great Gatsby* about how men and women communicate and respond to each other. Marriage, as he depicts it, is certainly no blissful state, but rather a constant and manipulative struggle of opposing forces. Couples seem to be defined by their suspicions, their tendencies toward deceit, mutual physical and psychological abuses, and insecurities. His notorious on-again, off-again relationship with Zelda and their shared destructiveness gave him much grist from which to craft his agonized depictions of human relationships. Gatsby, we learn, took Daisy "unscrupulously and ravenously." And in the section quoted here Carraway refers to Jordan Baker as being "incurably dishonest." The complexities in the relations between men and women are always a topic that book club members can sink their teeth into.

It also helps, when discussing a book like *The Great Gatsby*, to know that Fitzgerald himself grew up within a privileged class of American society that had access to such institutions as, for example, Princeton. Therefore, when he introduces characters who also belong to that social class, as well as those who wish to enter it, he speaks from his own personal experience. Perhaps more importantly, when he exposes that social class for its short-comings, he once again enjoys a privileged perspective. An author must intimately know that which he or she wishes to criticize.

Fitzgerald has been called "the voice of his generation." If so, that generation did not have a very optimistic outlook on such social institutions as marriage. You may want to ask what such a comment implies, challenging the assumptions behind it. A close reading of Chapter III will reveal many instances of this disillusionment. This topic can easily lead into a very meaningful comparative discussion about how authors of our own era see and describe human relationships, in books such as, for example, Margaret Atwood's *Life Before Man* or Alice Munro's *The Love of a Good Woman*.

Writers of Fitzgerald's status cannot help but be defined by and help to define their era and their generation. Fitzgerald was known as the voice of the Jazz Age, and *The Great Gatsby* is the novel in which he most famously defines that era. Whether or not the Jazz Age was exactly as Fitzgerald imagined it, it is interesting that his depiction of it has almost completely defined it for us. What we are left with is a fictional representation of a society of excess, irresponsibility, over-indulgence and, ultimately, disillu-sionment, as is evident in the above chapter: "There was dancing now on the canvas in the garden, old men pushing young girls backward in eternal graceless circles, superior couples holding each other tortuously, fashionably and keeping in the corners— and a great number of single girls dancing individualistically or relieving the orchestra for a moment of the burden of the banjo or the traps...The moon had risen higher, and floating in the Sound was a triangle of silver scales, trembling a little to the stiff, tinny, drip of the banjoes on the lawn."

It is always helpful to read such quotes aloud and ask fellow book club members what such language evokes in them. From this lush quote, members may get a sense of a generation defined by its energetic and ecstatic music, by the physical tensions between the sexes, by the "tortuous" qualities of its festivities.

Once you have established not only the author's personal history but also his or her publishing history as well, you and your fellow club members can discuss how this one work fits into the broader context of that author's oeuvre. Sometimes, when discussing an author's first or only work, this may be more difficult, but the book as an isolated event might itself become a worthwhile topic of conversation. For example, the great American novelist Ralph Ellison wrote only one published novel, *Invisible Man* (1952), and the fact that he then stopped publishing fiction makes a discussion of his writing career even more fascinating.

Ask your fellow members what consistencies they detect among Fitzgerald's different novels. Even this brief synopsis of his other works suggests certain thematic patterns that informed his creative development. In other words, sometimes knowing the thematic concerns of other works can add insight into the work you are discussing, whether you have actually read those other works or not. Like *The Great Gatsby*, some of his other works addressed such issues as the moral, emotional, spiritual, physiological and psychological disintegration of the individual.

Of course, not every biographical detail of the author is directly relevant to the book you are discussing. *The Great Gatsby* is not a memoir or an autobiography. Drawing too many connections between an author's life and the characters he or she creates can limit a full exploration of the design, themes and pleasures of the work in front of you. When it is relevant, use the biographical information as a helpful guide. Don't interpret the information as a map to all the roads, cities and topographical features of the book you're discussing.

The Root of All Evil? Character, Theme and Symbolism in *The Great Gatsby*

One of the reasons why we chose *The Great Gatsby* as our sample book is because, of all the books that we have read, few have more themes of universal appeal than Fitzgerald's masterpiece. Although it is set in a very specific historical moment and place, it remains a favourite, decade after decade, because each subsequent generation of readers recognizes the characters and events in their own world. Most recently the book was listed as the second most important and popular book of the decade in both the controversial Modern Library list and *The Globe and Mail*'s informal survey, both published in the summer of 1998. (The number-one choice, in both lists, was Joyce's *Ulysses*, but we thought that we would give you a break and stick with the number-two novel, which is a little more accessible.)

It would be difficult for any group discussing *The Great Gatsby* not to begin its thematic analysis of the book by focusing on Fitzgerald's depictions of Jay Gatsby's tremendous wealth. Even in the first paragraph of Chapter III of the book, in which Fitzgerald's legendary description of Gatsby's parties begins, we are given continuous references to material items that provide us with a sense of excessive and almost inconceivable wealth in the 1920s or today: champagne, motor boats, aquaplanes, Rolls-Royces, servants. The excess of Gatsby's life builds momentum as the chapter continues, where we read about the lushness of the setting, the catering, the music, the guests, the host and, perhaps most important, Nick Carraway's reaction to it all.

Of course, the depiction of wealth is not in itself a theme of the book, but there are many themes that can be culled from the observation that Fitzgerald is determined to give us in his very clear depiction of this lifestyle. The first thematic question that might be asked is whether Fitzgerald intends for us to see this excess as positive. Is he simply drawing us in, seducing us with all this luxury and beauty in order, ultimately, to expose this world for what it really is and to pull the rug out from under us? Knowing as we do that the novel ends tragically with death and disillusionment, it is a safe bet to say that the seductive wealth of this chapter is not, ultimately, beneficial. What are some of the ways that Fitzgerald brings us to this realization?

Although Fitzgerald begins his description by suggesting that Gatsby possesses everything money can buy, it is not long before some questions of the character's authenticity begin to arise. As Nick appears at the party, he tells us that "I believe…I was one of the few guests who had actually been invited." Suddenly the reader is left with a sense that there is a discrepancy between appearance and reality; where one would normally expect parties to be thrown for friends, here the host may not even know his guests. From a close examination of lines such as this, the members of your group might question whether there is a certain degree of theatricality to this wealth and these parties: rather than enjoying the company of his own acquaintances, Gatsby's wealth enables him to collect people and put on a show. The first theme that might arise, then, is that of appearance versus reality in questions of wealth.

Other quotations from this same chapter, which could or should be read aloud by the group member leading the discussion, help to sustain this suspicion. For example, in discussing Gatsby's origins, Jordan Baker tells Nick that "...he told me once that he was an Oxford man," but then comments, "However, I don't believe it." From this, the group may be left with a feeling that Gatsby's world is more illusion than reality. This point is underscored when the "stout, middle-aged man with enormous owl-eyed spectacles" expresses to Nick his absolute amazement at the fact that the books in Gatsby's library are actually real: "'It's a bona fide piece of printed matter. It fooled me. This fella's a regular Belasco. It's a triumph. What thoroughness! What realism! Knew when to stop, though—didn't cut the pages." In reading such sections aloud, the group, searching together for predominant themes, might realize that everyone suspects that Gatsby and his wealth possess a degree of artifice, and they are amazed when there is actually any substance behind him. This tells us that there is a degree of falseness not only to Gatsby, but also to the society that feeds off his spending.

From this sort of realization there are a number of directions in which discussions can go. Is there, for example, a suggestion that wealth itself is merely an illusion, behind which there is very little substance? If this is so, then is it only a matter of time before this illusion is exposed? *The Great Gatsby* is a good novel to build this discussion upon, because it is evident that Fitzgerald wanted to show us a series of characters with money (or at least an opulent lifestyle) who are eventually revealed to possess little substance behind their false facades. This, of course, can easily lead to a more general discussion on how members of the group see money and the role that it plays in our lives.

From here, it is not difficult for your group to begin talking about what *The Great Gatsby* says about the class orientation of our society (another theme that may be applied to virtually any discussion of any book). When Jordan Baker begins to doubt whether Jay Gatsby actually attended Oxford, we realize that there is a privileged class in this world to which Jay Gatsby wishes to belong, and which we doubt will ever accept him, no matter how hard he tries. Certainly, all club members will have an experience of not belonging to a specific social group at some point (even if they do, now, belong to your book club, an exclusive group indeed!).

This observation can lead to discussions of other themes. First, what does the class structure look like in the novel and how does that class structure compare to our own society? Think, for example, of the descriptions of "East Egg" and "West Egg" at the beginning of *The Great Gatsby* and how Nick Carraway tells us, from the onset, that there is a space in the society where only those who were born with money could belong.

Once the theme of the class orientation of the novel is brought out, there is no limit to the discussions that can arise. For example, is the class structure of the novel partially responsible for Jay Gatsby's death (in that he is ultimately destroyed by his inability to join that privileged class) or should he be held responsible for desiring something that, ultimately, holds little value? Is his passion for Daisy the result of his wanting to join the privileged class or does he attempt to join that class as a way of earning access to her? These thematic issues help draw readers further into the novel, and ultimately generate great debate, including such issues as whether class structures still play as great a role in our lives and our society. Is it still impossible for an outsider like Jay Gatsby to penetrate that invisible barrier between those who are "old money" and those who are "nouveau riche"?

In this kind of thematic discussion, numerous related debates are implied. Gatsby is an outsider to the world he is trying to enter, through excessive spending. Why is he an outsider? Well, we learn at one point that he had changed his name from James Gatz to Jay Gatsby. Why would he want to do so if there were not an ethnic past that he was trying to shed in order to integrate better into the privileged circle? This leads the discussion into the very challenging question of how outsiders are seen and treated in our society (yet another question that may be applied repeatedly to virtually any literary work). In this case, Gatsby is used for what he can offer monetarily, but he does not realize that he will never be able to purchase that which he is trying to buy. Again, does he bring this on himself or is Fitzgerald implicating the entire society he is writing about? Is this still the case today or, with time, has high society changed to permit access to those from a wider variety of backgrounds? (While you are reading books that were written or set in the past, it is always useful to compare that historical setting to the present day in order to gain further insight.)

Another theme that is implied in this discussion is that of how men and women treat each other in relationships. (This is another thematic question that can be raised in challenging ways in discussions of many different works.) Gatsby is trying to gain entry into privileged society in order to win Daisy's heart. He does manage to accomplish this, but, ultimately, he must lose out to Daisy's husband, the philandering Tom Buchanan. Apparently, because Gatsby was an outsider, he never had a chance to begin with, but instead, like the Wilsons, he is simply a pawn used within the span of the novel for the amusement of the wealthy. This issue can lead your group to a number of different and challenging questions. Did Gatsby love Daisy because of what she represented (wealth) or did he attempt to acquire and display great wealth as a way of winning her? Either way, this can open up numerous debates, depending on how the members of your group feel about such topics, and how they choose to back up their arguments within the group setting.

Perhaps the most important aspect of discussing themes in your book club is that they are usually general enough to move effortlessly into broader debates about which everyone will have an opinion and in which everyone can participate. Before the club meets, it is very easy (particularly if everyone has e-mail) to distribute a set of thematic questions. In relation to *The Great Gatsby*, you could begin with broad questions such as:

✳ What does money represent to Gatsby?

✳ How can we tell that there is a discrepancy between appearance and reality in the novel?

✳ What is it about the high class of American society that appeals to Gatsby?

✳ How can we anticipate that Gatsby and Daisy's love affair will end in tragedy?

✳ The owl-eyed man suggests that characters in the story are being watched. Where else do we see this? What is the significance of this watchful presence?

You can send out these questions a few days before your meeting to allow your fellow book club members to ponder them, whether you are the scheduled leader or are just sending them "unprovoked." You might be amazed at how profound their observations can be. (The first time that we tried circulating such questions among the members of our own book club by e-mail, we received complaints like: "Oh my God, we're back in school!" But these questions led to a great discussion and soon became the standard for all meetings.)

Honesty Is the Best Policy (Well at Least Sometimes): The Role of the Narrator and Fitzgerald's Writing Style

Although there are times in *The Great Gatsby* when we sense that we are almost reading a work of history, or at least an objective account of another person's life, we are, of course, only reading one person's very selective, idiosyncratic tale remembered long after it happened. As readers we must remember that Nick Carraway, the person telling us the story, like all narrators, is not an impartial observer, nor is he a surrogate for the author. In any book it is important to clarify at the beginning of your discussion who is telling the story and why that person is telling it in that manner, and then to decide if you are going to believe him or her. Although we cannot discuss all the many different permutations that authors have to tell you the story—either fiction or non-fiction—it is important to provide you with a few guideposts.

It may be that the book you are reading is told in the third person, as though the narrator knows everything—the actions, words, thoughts, secrets—about all the characters in the book. This mode of storytelling is common throughout literature because it gives the author ultimate licence to tell you anything he or she would like you to know. This is not to say that the author of the book is impartial or to be believed in everything he or she presents to you, humble reader. Fiction is fiction, after all, and one of the joys of a good read is that it transports us into a created world, rather than numbs us into stupefying sleep with the facts of the mundane world around us. Authors are people, too, and sometimes they like to have fun with their characters and their readers. Why shouldn't they throw in a few literary stumbling blocks or a few intellectual mazes? It makes readers that much more attentive and provides them with challenges to figure out on their own. This isn't a technical manual you're reading, after all...

In a novel narrated in the third person, it is always fun for the group to challenge the information provided by the narrator, but in a novel told by one of its characters, it is absolutely necessary. If the story is told in the first person, the narrator is the filter through which all information passes to you. At times this stream of information may seem to be impartially told, as in Michael Ondaatje's *The English Patient* or Margaret Laurence's *The Stone*

Angel, and at others it seems that as a reader you have to be forever on your guard to establish what is believable and what is not. The narrator in J. D. Salinger's *The Catcher in the Rye* is one of the most famous examples of this very selective voice, and Holden Caulfield shows no desire at all to be informative about all aspects that the reader may be interested in: "If you really want to hear about it, the first thing you'll really want to know is where I was born, and what my lousy childhood was like, and how my parents were occupied and all before they had me, and all that David Copperfield kind of crap..." From that opening sentence we know we are going to get a harsh and completely biased look at a troubled life.

The narrator of any book is not the author. He or she or it is merely a very particular mirror—often distorted or coloured or warped—that reflects to us the action of the book. We say "it" because there are many examples of non-human things that tell the story of the book, including the Governor General's Award–winning book *Shakespeare's Dog* by Leon Rooke (told by, well, you know who). In Robertson Davies's *Murther & Walking Spirits*, the "I" of the book is killed off in the very first sentence and the "walking spirit" takes over from there.

In *The Great Gatsby*, Nick Carraway is the lens through which we see Jay Gatsby and come to know him. Often the first-person narrator would have the reader believe that he or she is honest, and Nick is no exception. As he says in the final sentence of the excerpt above: "Every one suspects himself of at least one of the cardinal virtues, and this is mine: I am one of the few honest people that I have ever known."

Yet why, the members of your book club should ask, should we as readers believe him or trust him? The story that he tells us has been cobbled together from things that others tell him, including snippets from Jordan Baker, Gatsby himself and the gossipy girls he meets at the party, who love to tell stories about Gatsby's mysterious past. In addition there is his own naturally faulty memory and the various documents he has kept, among them the "time-table" now so old that it is "disintegrating at its folds" as he tells us at the beginning of Chapter IV. But the most important influence on the story is his own ego, his own conception of himself and his place in the world.

From the pretensions of the opening sentences of the book to his mention of the "vague understanding that had to be tactfully broken off before I was set free," and on to the final thoughts of the book—where he makes grand, sweeping statements about aesthetic contemplation and history—we are in the hands of a person intent on giving us not a historical account of an individual or a set of actions, but rather an insight into his own character. The book is Carraway's account and we as readers must navigate through his delusions and fantasies and inconsistencies in order to arrive at information about America in the 1920s or Jay Gatsby or the tragedies that await us toward the end of the book.

One of the things most evident about Nick throughout the novel is his vulnerability, his willingness to be led along by other people in his opinions and conclusions. In the chapter quoted here, just after he meets Gatsby, he pesters Jordan to tell him anything she knows about Gatsby. At first she mentions Gatsby went to Oxford and immediately a "dim background started to take shape behind him [Gatsby], but at her next remark it faded away. 'However, I don't believe it.' " His imagination seems to travel in the wake left by Jordan's words, just as they have followed the trials and turns of other people's opinions and speculations when they talk about Gatsby and his unknown past.

A few pages later Nick states: "Reading over what I have written so far I see that I have given the impression that the events of three nights several weeks apart were all that absorbed me. On the contrary they were merely casual events in a crowded summer and, until much later, they absorbed me infinitely less than my personal affairs." In reading such self-referential narrative passages aloud in a group discussion, one could suggest that this is indeed a curious statement from someone obsessed with Gatsby and the high life of such parties that would have been until then completely foreign. For "merely casual events" they have taken on a very rich and textured existence, and seem to have completely absorbed Nick's imagination, body and soul. It is also a rather bizarre statement if we consider that earlier in the book Gatsby has been either lionized by Nick or referred to as someone who "represented everything for which I have an unaffected scorn."

Upon reading such statements, the group may have the impression that Nick is a voice and a force to be marvelled at, to be enjoyed and to be followed as he leads us into the tale of Gatsby. As Tony Tanner says in the introduction to the Penguin edition of the book, we get Nick's "hypothesizing, speculating, imagining—and perhaps suppressing, recasting, fantasizing." As with other narrators you encounter in other books, Nick does not have to be believed or trusted, any more than we would believe or trust anyone else making up a story in a way that makes him or her seem to be the moral centre of an otherwise corrupt world.

Pro and Con-text: Discussing Books Within Their Historical Context and Setting

Another important aspect of every book that should never be completely neglected in book club discussions is the historical context in which a book was written. Like gathering biographical information on the author, this may require some degree of research on the part of a volunteer in the group, but not too much, since in most cases group members can offer general reflections on their sense of the period (let's face it, we all have a vague sense of what the 1950s must have been like from watching "Happy Days" and of what the 1850s must have been like from the musical *Oliver*...er, on second thought, maybe we should be challenging those notions). Five minutes on the Internet and you should be able to gather up all the material you will need to get this discussion going.

When it comes to discussing historical context, though, you should be careful. When discussing *The Great Gatsby*, for example, it is obvious that we are talking about the 1920s. But what if we were discussing a novel set in the 1920s written by an author working in the 1950s? Or by an author working today? Would we be talking about the same 1920s, or would we be talking about a completely different version of the 1920s? Why did this author decide to return to this historical era? Is it an attempt to use another period to comment on his or her own historical moment? By the same token, are all futuristic science-fiction stories really about the time frame in which they were written? These are all interesting and challenging questions, and can guide a book group into some highly charged areas.

It is absolutely necessary to discuss, at least at some point in your book club meeting, a novel like *The Great Gatsby* within the context of the historical setting in which it was written. The style, the music, the money and the excess of the 1920s, as we envision them, are very much alive in our imagination, and in Fitzgerald's novel, the feeling of the era leaps off the page: "Suddenly one of the gypsies in trembling opal seizes a cocktail out of the air, dumps it down for courage and moving her hands like Frisco dances out alone on the canvas platform. A momentary hush; the orchestra leader varies his rhythm obligingly for her and there is a burst of chatter as the erroneous news goes around that she is Gilda Gray's understudy from the "Follies." The party has begun."

The first question that the group can ask when reading aloud a passage like this is: What is the sense of this era that we are given in this novel? Our first response is fairly obvious. By any standards, it is a time of wealth, of lushness, of excess, when people seemed first and foremost interested in a good time. In the above quote, Fitzgerald seems to be describing the flapper, one of the great icons of the 1920s, the thin woman with short straight hair, a short fringed skirt, too much make-up and pearls, who perfected legendary bent-kneed dance steps. Together with the popularizing of jazz music and a runaway stock market, the flapper defined that decade as a period of fun and fantasy.

But the book club conversation should not end here with the more common observations, no matter what book you happen to be discussing. There are ways to take this conversation in very meaningful directions with a few more challenging questions. For example, once your club has observed the world that Fitzgerald describes in the section quoted here, someone in the group could (and should) ask whether there is a sense that, even for Fitzgerald, all is not as it appears—is he subverting his own description? A question like this forces the group to examine the words more closely. Why, for instance, does he tell us that "the erroneous news goes around that she is Gilda Gray's understudy"? Clearly there is a lack of authenticity in the entire scene. Not only is the woman not who people think she is, but the woman they think she is, is in fact the understudy of an actual celebrity. On closer inspection, it appears that Fitzgerald invokes this only to suggest, in subtle ways, that the whole thing is a grand illusion, and if it is an illusion then it may eventually be exposed as such. In this description, then, a great deal about the novel as a whole is uncovered. In virtually any good work of literature, such insights can be revealed when your club challenges its own initial assumptions.

There are a number of other good questions that a book club can ask when addressing the historical context of a novel that should enable group members to move together toward some great insights. If you are discussing a novel as historically significant to an era as *The Great Gatsby* (other examples are *The Scarlet Letter, Great Expectations, The Canterbury Tales, To Kill a Mockingbird, Little Women, For Whom the Bell Tolls, The Bonfire of the Vanities*—you get the picture), a good question to ask might be whether these works are defined by the historical moment about which they were written or whether they define our perception today of that moment. For example, for most of us, whether we have read *The Great Gatsby* or not, we probably imagine the 1920s looking pretty much like Fitzgerald's version of it. That is because Fitzgerald's novel is the embodiment of the period. Even though there are probably an infinite number of illustrations of what the decade must have been like (picture an immigrant novel or an African American novel set in the southern U.S.), his is the one that has survived. It has formed our mythology. Is this because his novel was the most accurate, or because this is the version with which we are most comfortable for some reason? Such questions can provoke powerful debates among book club members, particularly if you are discussing a novel from a time that people can still remember.

Another good question to ask about any novel from another historical period is: How does this period, or this depiction of it, contrast with our own historical moment? In the case of a novel like *The Great Gatsby*, there should be no shortage of debate in response to such a question. One person in the group will likely suggest that, since the novel is set before the Great Depression or the Second World War, there is still a sense of innocence in Fitzgerald's world, where characters can embrace the excitement of the moment without the same degree of wariness that we have today. Other club members might disagree, arguing that Fitzgerald, in giving us this seemingly innocent world, was also hinting at a profound sense of impending doom beneath the surface, and that the innocence was never really there at any moment. This debate can be quite productive, since everyone present should have their own opinion on the topic.

Of course, the degree to which your group delves into the complexities of discussing the novel's historical context depends on your companions' involvement in the text, but having the right questions in your arsenal can make all the difference.

Tools of the Trade: Other Sources

There are a variety of other sources that your club may consider as a complement to *The Great Gatsby*. As with other great writers, an industry has grown up around F. Scott Fitzgerald that sustains a great number of academic and non-academic pursuits (if not a great number of academic careers). Most notable are the large number of biographies and memoirs that deal with Fitzgerald, his travels, his books, his relationship with Zelda and, as one biography puts it, his "homes and haunts."

Matthew J. Bruccoli is perhaps the best-known writer and scholar on Fitzgerald's work and has produced one of the most important biographies on the writer: *Some Sort of Epic Grandeur: The Life of F. Scott Fitzgerald.* He has also produced, together with Scottie Fitzgerald Smith and Joan P. Kerr, a lively work that provides local colour to the novel: *The Romantic Egoists: A Pictorial Autobiography from the Scrapbooks and Albums of F. Scott Fitzgerald and Zelda Fitzgerald.*

There is also an assortment of books by other writers on their relationship with Fitzgerald, including Morley Callaghan's book *That Summer in Paris,* and Ernest Hemingway's *A Moveable Feast.* Both Callaghan and Hemingway provide intimate details on the life of talented, struggling writers coping with social restrictions, their own intellectual and physical urges, and the desire to provide a lasting record of their times.

If you are interested in critical essays or books on Fitzgerald and his work, there are dozens to choose from. Among the most helpful are the following: John B. Chambers's *The Novels of F. Scott Fitzgerald*, Harold Bloom's collection of essays, *F. Scott Fitzgerald's The Great Gatsby*, Alfred Kazin's collection entitled *F. Scott Fitzgerald: The Man and His Work*, and Henry Dan Piper's collection, *Fitzgerald's The Great Gatsby: The Novel, the Critics, the Background*. In all of these books you will find insights into the novel that will help you explore the many intricacies of this seminal work of literature.

Don't forget, however, that not all critics have been insightful or helpful in their assessment of *The Great Gatsby*. Among the first reviews of the book were the following negative ones: "A little slack, a little soft, more than a little artificial. *The Great Gatsby* falls into the class of negligible novels" from the *Springfield Republican*, and this angry review from the *Saturday Review of Literature*: "Mr. F. Scott Fitzgerald deserves a good shaking...*The Great Gatsby* is an absurd story, whether considered as romance, melodrama, or plain record of New York high life."

The fun thing about reading criticism on the book that you are discussing is that you will often discover that you, as a group, have found things in the book that no one else has seen. That is one of the marvellous things about truly great literature: it goes on revealing itself in new ways to each new reader.

If you grow tired of reading the critical work on Fitzgerald, you can always rent and view as a group the movie version of *The Great Gatsby*, made in 1974 and starring Robert Redford and Mia Farrow. The movie gives a very good visual sense of the age and the ecstatic energy of the lifestyle but cannot do justice to the depth and richness of the novel or the subtleties of Nick's narration. The only place to find those is, of course, in the book itself.

Truth or

Consequences:

Sample

Non-fiction

Reading and

Discussion

> *Our memoirs are card-indexes consulted,*
> *and then put back in disorder by authorities*
> *whom we do not control.*
>
> CYRIL CONNOLLY, *"UNQUIET GRAVE"*

The Truth, the Whole Truth and Nothing but the Truth (Sort Of)

Your book club has now been in full swing for six months or so and everyone seems to have enjoyed most of the discussions and the intellectual sparring that has taken place. Your group has managed to choose, read and debate six novels, some of which many of you enjoyed and a few of which did not meet everyone's expectations. Lately, though, you and several other members have been starting to suspect that the group has lost its momentum. While you all enjoy the entertainment value of a good story, some of you are looking for something to break up the monotony of discussing fiction month after month. You are finding that people usually bring to the table, if not the same opinions, then at least the same general attitudes toward entering an author's fictional world. The same subjects and the same complaints are starting to recur and, especially at the end of your meetings, the excitement is starting to wane. This is probably the perfect time to turn your attention to a couple of good works of non-fiction.

The natural tendency for most book groups is to choose novels or collections of stories and to ignore the many worthwhile non-fiction books that are available for discussion. Although you probably began your book club with the idea that the books were primarily going to be a source of entertainment or escape, there is no reason why you shouldn't feel that you can learn something along the way as well. The members of your club have common interests that logically draw them toward non-fictional works on certain topics. For example, some book clubs, particularly around income-tax time, might want to read a book related to the topic of personal finances. During the summer, the group might decide to read something about gardening, travel, baseball or affordable activities for children. In the winter, it could be suggested that the group read one of the hundreds of books available on seasonal affective disorder or Martha Stewart's books of Christmas decorations and cooking. There may be a new biography on a writer a few of you have read (perhaps even one of the authors you have read in your book club). The ideas really are limitless. The non-fiction book list that we provide later in this book will give you 100 possibilities to get you thinking and reading. As one of our friends in another book club told us: "Our group was overwhelmed when we finally thought about all the great books we were avoiding in our club. One member suggested we read *A History of Reading* by Alberto Manguel. And when we got to it our group loved it. There wasn't much to argue about or disagree over, but the book is full of fascinating information for those who read and love books. Manguel's book got us thinking about reading itself in all sorts of new ways."

There is no doubt that non-fiction books are different from novels, and in trying to discuss them you will be presented with different challenges. In some ways, fiction books are easier to discuss because they tell a story, they introduce you to characters, they create a fictional world that has some relationship with our world. For these reasons, novels will inevitably evoke in us an emotional, intellectual and even sympathetic reaction.

Rather than telling us a story, works of non-fiction are, in theory, telling us facts, and they are written in such a way as to suggest that we are meant to accept these facts as entirely reliable. We don't want to pick up a book in which the author is giving us helpful hints on travelling through Greece and have to question whether the islands really look the way the author is describing them, whether the food really tastes as good, whether the people really are as charming.

Sometimes the best joy is not having to experience what the author is writing about. In his marvellously rich and difficult memoir *The Worst Journey in the World*, Apsley Cherry-Garrard, one of the youngest members of Scott's British Antarctic expedition, states: "Polar exploration is at once the cleanest and most isolated way of having a bad time which has yet been devised. It is the only form of adventure in which you put on your clothes at Michaelmas and keep them on until Christmas, and, save for a layer of the natural grease of the body, find them as clean as though they were new. It is more lonely than London, more secluded than a monastery, and the post comes but once a year." Put simply, most people would rather read about such "adventures" than go on them.

All of this tells us why non-fiction books are great to read, but the question still remains, would they generate good conversations at book club meetings? How can the club discuss them with the same degree of critical insight and passion as they would a novel? A good book club discussion of a work of non-fiction must address not only the subject of the book, but the author's unique shaping of the topic as well. In certain respects, the work of non-fiction is as much about the author's own way of seeing the topic as it is about the topic itself. In Susanna Moodie's classic autobiographical book, *Roughing It in the Bush*, she describes her experience of being one of the very early settlers in Canada. On first impression, it might be difficult to imagine how this book could possibly generate a good book club discussion, since today we share so little in common with Moodie, and therefore we might assume that we have to take everything that she tells us as absolute truth. There are many different written accounts of similar experiences of settling in Canada (including a famous one by Moodie's own sister, Catherine Parr Traill, and one by her husband, John Dunbar Moodie), and all of these accounts are quite different. As we look more closely at Moodie's work, we see how extensively the "facts" she gives us are moulded by her own character, and how the "truth" of the work is profoundly affected by the way she chooses to present it to us, by her own personal agenda, and by her need to tell a story, even while she tells us a version of the truth.

ROUGHING IT IN THE BUSH BY SUSANNA MOODIE:

Excerpts from Chapter X, "Brian, The Still-Hunter"

It was early day. I was alone in the old shanty, preparing breakfast, and now and then stirring the cradle with my foot, when a tall, thin, middle-aged man walked into the house, followed by two large, strong dogs.

Placing the rifle he had carried on his shoulder in a corner of the room, he advanced to the hearth, and, without speaking, or seemingly looking at me, lighted his pipe and commenced smoking. The dogs, after growling and snapping at the cat, who had not given the strangers a very courteous reception, sat down on the hearth-stone on either side of their taciturn master, eyeing him from time to time, as if long habit had made them understand all his motions. There was a great contrast between the dogs. The one was a brindled bulldog of the largest size, a most formidable and powerful brute; the other a staghound, tawny, deep-chested, and strong-limbed. I regarded the man and his hairy companions with silent curiosity.

He was between forty and fifty years of age; his head, nearly bald, was studded at the sides with strong, coarse, black curling hair. His features were high, his complexion brightly dark, and his eyes, in size, shape, and colour, greatly resembling the eyes of a hawk. The face itself was sorrowful and taciturn; and his thin, compressed lips looked as if they were not much accustomed to smile, or often to unclose to hold social communion with any one. He stood at the side of the huge hearth, silently smoking, his eyes bent on the fire, and now and then he patted the heads of his dogs, reproving their exuberant expression of attachment, with "Down, Musie; down, Chance!"

"A cold, clear morning," said I, in order to attract his attention and draw him into conversation.

A nod, without raising his head, or withdrawing his eyes from the fire, was his only answer; and, turning from my unsociable guest, I took up the baby, who just then awoke, sat down on a low stool by the table, and began feeding her. During this operation, I once or twice caught the stranger's hawk-eye fixed upon me and the child, but word spoke he none; and presently, after whistling to his dogs, he resumed his gun, and strode out.

When Moodie and Monaghan came in to breakfast, I told them what a strange visitor I had had; and Moodie laughed at my vain attempt to induce him to talk.

"He is a strange being," I said; "I must find out who and what he is."

In the afternoon an old soldier, called Layton, who had served during the American war, and got a grant of land about a mile in the rear of our location, came in to trade for a cow. Now, this Layton was a perfect ruffian, a man whom no one liked, and whom all feared. He was a deep drinker, a great swearer, in short, a perfect reprobate, who never cultivated his land, but went jobbing about from farm to farm, trading horses and cattle, and cheating in a pettifogging way. Uncle Joe had employed him to sell Moodie a young heifer, and he had brought her over for him to look at. When he came in to be paid, I described the stranger of the morning; and as I knew that he was familiar with every one in the neighbourhood, I asked if he knew him.

"No one should know him better than myself," he said; "'tis old Brian B—, the still-hunter, and a near neighbour of your'n. A sour, morose, queer chap he is, and as mad as a March hare! He's from Lancashire, in England, and came to this country some twenty years ago, with his wife, who was a pretty young lass in those days, and slim enough then, though she's so awful fleshy now. He had lots of money, too, and he bought four hundred acres of land, just at the corner of the concession line, where it meets the main road. And excellent land it is; and a better farmer, while he stuck to his business, never went into the bush, for it was all bush here then. He was a dashing, handsome fellow, too, and did not hoard the money, either; he loved his pipe and his pot too well; and at last he left off farming, and gave himself to them altogether. Many a jolly booze he and I have had, I can tell you. Brian was an awful passionate man, and, when the liquor was in, and the wit was out, as savage and as quarrelsome as a bear. At such times there was no one but Ned Layton dared go near him. We once had a pitched battle, in which I was conqueror, and ever arter he yielded a sort of sulky obedience to all I said to him. Arter being on the spree for a week or two, he would take fits of remorse, and return home to his wife; would fall down at her knees, and ask her forgiveness, and cry like a child. At other times he would hide himself up in the woods, and steal home at night, and get what he wanted out of the pantry, without speaking a word to any one. He went on with these pranks for some years, till he took a fit of the blue devils.

" 'Come away, Ned, to the — lake, with me,' said he; 'I am weary of my life, and I want a change.'

" 'Shall we take the fishing-tackle?' says I. 'The black bass are in prime season, and F— will lend us the old canoe. He's got some capital rum up from Kingston. We'll fish all day, and have a spree at night.'

" 'It's not to fish I'm going,' says he.

" 'To shoot, then? I've bought Rockwood's new rifle.'

" 'It's neither to fish nor to shoot, Ned: it's a new game I'm going to try; so come along.'

"Well, to the — lake we went. The day was very hot, and our path lay through the woods, and over those scorching plains, for eight long miles. I thought I should have dropped by the way; but during our long walk my companion never opened his lips. He strode on before me, at a half-run, never once turning his head.

" 'The man must be the devil!' says I, 'and accustomed to a warmer place, or he must feel this. Hollo, Brian! Stop there! Do you mean to kill me?'

" 'Take it easy,' says he; 'you'll see another day arter this— I've business on hand and cannot wait.'

"Well, on we went, at the same awful rate, and it was midday when we got to the little tavern on the lake shore, kept by one F—, who had a boat for the convenience of strangers who came to visit the place. Here we got our dinner, and a glass of rum to wash it down. But Brian was moody, and to all my jokes he only returned a sort of grunt; and while I was talking with F—, he steps out, and a few minutes arter we saw him crossing the lake in the old canoe.

" 'What's the matter with Brian?' says F—; 'all does not seem right with him, Ned. You had better take the boat and look arter him.'

" 'Pooh!' says I; 'he's often so, and grows so glum now-a-days that I will cut his acquaintance altogether if he does not improve.'

" 'He drinks awful hard,' says F—; 'may be he's got a fit of the delirium-tremulous. There is no telling what he may be up to at this minute.'

"My mind misgave me too, so I e'en takes the oars, and pushes out, right upon Brian's track; and, by the Lord Harry! if I did not find him, upon my landing on the opposite shore, lying wallowing in his blood, with his throat cut. 'Is that you, Brian?' says I, giving him a kick with my foot, to see if he was alive or dead. 'What on earth tempted you to play me and F— such a dirty, mean trick, as to go and stick yourself like a pig, bringing such a discredit upon the house?—and you so far from home and those who should nurse you?'

"I was so mad with him, that (saving your presence, ma'am) I swore awfully, and called him names that would be ondacent to repeat here; but he only answered with groans and a horrid gurgling in his throat. 'It's a-choking you are,' said I, 'but you shan't have your own way and die so easily either, if I can punish you by keeping you alive.' So I just turned him upon his stomach, with his head down the steep bank; but he still kept choking and growing black in the face."

Layton then detailed some particulars of his surgical practice which it is not necessary to repeat. He continued:

"I bound up his throat with my handkerchief, and took him neck and heels, and threw him into the bottom of the boat. Presently he came to himself a little, and sat up in the boat; and—would you believe it?—made several attempts to throw himself in the water. 'This will not do,' says I; 'you've done mischief enough already by cutting your weasand! If you dare to try that again, I will kill you with the oar.' I held it up to threaten him; he was scared, and lay down as quiet as a lamb. I put my foot upon his breast. 'Lie still, now! or you'll catch it.' He looked piteously at me; he could not speak, but his eyes seemed to say, 'Have pity upon me, Ned; don't kill me.'

"Yes, ma'am, this man, who had just cut his throat, and twice arter that tried to drown himself, was afraid that I should knock him on the head and kill him. Ha! ha! I shall never forget the work that F— and I had with him arter I got him up to the house.

"The doctor came, and sewed up his throat; and his wife— poor crittur!—came to nurse him. Bad as he was, she was mortal fond of him! He lay there, sick and unable to leave his bed, for three months, and did nothing but pray to God to forgive him, for he thought the devil would surely have him for cutting his own throat; and when he got about again, which is now twelve years ago, he left off drinking entirely, and wanders about the woods with his dogs, hunting. He seldom speaks to any one, and his wife's brother carries on the farm for the family. He is so shy of strangers that 'tis a wonder he came in here. The old wives are afraid of him; but you need not heed him—his troubles are to himself, he harms no one."

Layton departed, and left me brooding over the sad tale which he had told in such an absurd and jesting manner. It was evident from the account he had given of Brian's attempt at suicide, that the hapless hunter was not wholly answerable for his conduct—that he was a harmless maniac.

The next morning, at the very same hour, Brian again made his appearance; but instead of the rifle across his shoulder, a large stone jar occupied the place, suspended by a stout leather thong. Without saying a word, but with a truly benevolent smile that flitted slowly over his stern features, and lighted them up like a sunbeam breaking from beneath a stormy cloud, he advanced to the table, and unslinging the jar, set it down before me, and in a low and gruff, but by no means an unfriendly voice, said, "Milk, for the child," and vanished.

"How good it was of him! How kind!" I exclaimed, as I poured the precious gift of four quarts of pure new milk out into a deep pan. I had not asked him—had never said that the poor weanling wanted milk. It was the courtesy of a gentleman—of a man of benevolence and refinement.

For weeks did my strange, silent friend steal in, take up the empty jar, and supply its place with another replenished with milk. The baby knew his step, and would hold out her hands to him and cry, "Milk!" and Brian would stoop down and kiss her, and his two great dogs lick her face.

"Have you any children, Mr. B—?"

"Yes, five; but none like this."

"My little girl is greatly indebted to you for your kindness."

"She's welcome, or she would not get it. You are strangers; but I like you all. You look kind, and I would like to know more about you."

Moodie shook hands with the old hunter, and assured him that we should always be glad to see him. After this invitation, Brian became a frequent guest. He would sit and listen with delight to Moodie while he described to him elephant-hunting at the Cape, grasping his rifle in a determined manner, and whistling an encouraging air to his dogs. I asked him one evening what made him so fond of hunting.

" 'Tis the excitement," he said; "it drowns thought, and I love to be alone. I am sorry for the creatures, too, for they are free and happy; yet I am led by an instinct I cannot restrain to kill them. Sometimes the sight of their dying agonies recalls painful feelings, and then I lay aside the gun, and do not hunt for days. But 'tis fine to be alone with God in the great woods—to watch the sunbeams stealing through the thick branches, the blue sky breaking in upon you in patches, and to know that all is bright and shiny above you, in spite of the gloom that surrounds you."

After a long pause, he continued, with much solemn feeling in his look and tone:

"I lived a life of folly for years, for I was respectably born and educated, and had seen something of the world, perhaps more than was good, before I left home for the woods; and from the teaching I had received from kind relatives and parents I should have known how to have conducted myself better. But, madam, if we associate long with the depraved and ignorant, we learn to become even worse than they. I felt deeply my degradation—felt that I had become the slave to low vice, and, in order to emancipate myself from the hateful tyranny of evil passions, I did a very rash and foolish thing. I need not mention the manner in which I transgressed God's holy laws; all the neighbours know it, and must have told you long ago. I could have borne reproof, but they turned my sorrow into indecent jests, and, unable to bear their coarse ridicule, I made companions of my dogs and gun, and went forth into the wilderness. Hunting became a habit. I could no longer live without it, and it supplies the stimulant which I lost when I renounced the cursed whiskey-bottle.

"I remember the first hunting excursion I took alone in the forest. How sad and gloomy I felt! I thought that there was no creature in the world so miserable as myself. I was tired and hungry, and I sat down upon a fallen tree to rest. All was still as death around me, and I was fast sinking to sleep, when my attention was aroused by a long, wild cry. My dog, for I had not Chance then, and he's no hunter, pricked up his ears, but instead of answering with a bark of defiance, he crouched down, trembling, at my feet. 'What does this mean?' I cried, and I cocked my rifle and sprang upon the log. The sound came nearer upon the wind. It was like the deep baying of a pack of hounds in full cry. Presently a noble deer rushed past me, and fast upon his trail—I see them now, like so many black devils—swept by a pack of ten or fifteen large, fierce wolves, with fiery eyes and bristling hair, and paws that seemed hardly to touch the ground in their eager haste. I thought not of danger, for, with their prey in view, I was safe; but I felt every nerve within me tremble for the fate of the poor deer. The wolves gained upon him at every bound. A close thicket intercepted his path, and, rendered desperate, he turned at bay. His nostrils were dilated, and his eyes seemed to send forth long streams of light. It was wonderful to witness the courage of the beast. How bravely he repelled the attacks of his deadly enemies, how gallantly he tossed them to the right and left, and spurned them from beneath his hoofs; yet all his struggles were useless, and he was quickly overcome and torn to pieces by his ravenous foes. At that moment he seemed more unfortunate than even myself, for I could not see in what manner he had deserved his fate. All his speed and energy, his courage and fortitude, had been exerted in vain. I had tried to destroy myself; but he, with every effort vigorously made for self-preservation, was doomed to meet the fate he dreaded! Is God just to his creatures?"

My recollections of Brian seemed more particularly to concentrate in the adventures of one night, when I happened to be left alone, for the first time since my arrival in Canada. I cannot now imagine how I could have been such a fool as to give way for four-and-twenty hours to such childish fears; but so it was, and I will not disguise my weakness from my indulgent reader.

Moodie had bought a very fine cow of a black man, named Mollineux, for which he was to give twenty-seven dollars. The man lived twelve miles back in the woods, and one fine, frosty spring day—(don't smile at the term frosty, thus connected with the genial season of the year; the term is perfectly correct when applied to the Canadian spring, which, until the middle of May, is the most dismal season of the year)—he and John Monaghan took a rope and the dog, and sallied forth to fetch the cow home. Moodie said that they should be back by six o'clock in the evening, and charged me to have something cooked for supper when they returned, as he doubted not their long walk in the sharp air would give them a good appetite. This was during the time that I was without a servant, and living in old Mrs —'s shanty.

The day was so bright and clear, and Katie was so full of frolic and play, rolling upon the floor, or toddling from chair to chair, that the day passed on without my feeling remarkably lonely. At length the evening drew nigh, and I began to expect my husband's return, and to think of the supper that I was to prepare for his reception. The red heifer that we had bought of Layton, came lowing to the door to be milked, but I did not know how to milk in those days, and, besides this, I was terribly afraid of cattle. Yet, as I knew that milk would be required for the tea, I ran across the meadow to Mrs Joe, and begged that one of her girls would be so kind as to milk for me. My request was greeted with a rude burst of laughter from the whole set.

"If you can't milk," said Mrs Joe, "it's high time you should learn. My girls are above being helps."

"I would not ask you but as a great favour; I am afraid of cows."

"*Afraid of cows*! Lord bless the woman! A farmer's wife and afraid of cows!"

Here followed another laugh at my expense; and, indignant at the refusal of my first and last request, when they had all borrowed so much from me, I shut the inhospitable door, and returned home.

After many ineffectual attempts, I succeeded at last, and bore my half-pail of milk in triumph to the house. Yes! I felt prouder of that milk that many an author of the best thing he ever wrote, whether in verse or prose; and it was doubly sweet when I considered that I had procured it without being under any obligation to my ill-natured neighbours. I had learned a useful lesson of independence, to which in after years I had often again to refer. I fed little Katie and put her to bed, made the hot cakes for tea, boiled the potatoes, and laid the ham, cut in nice slices, in the pan, ready to cook the moment I saw the men enter the meadow, and arranged the little room with scrupulous care and neatness. A glorious fire was blazing on the hearth, and everything was ready for their supper, and I began to look out anxiously for their arrival.

The night had closed in cold and foggy, and I could no longer distinguish any object at more than a few yards from the door. Bringing in as much wood as I thought would last me for several hours, I closed the door; and for the first time in my life I found myself at night in a house entirely alone. Then I began to ask myself a thousand torturing questions as to the reason of their unusual absence. Had they lost their way in the woods? Could they have fallen in with wolves (one of my early bugbears)? Could any fatal accident have befallen them? I started up, opened the door, held my breath, and listened. The little brook lifted up its voice in loud, hoarse wailing, or mocked, in its babbling to the stones, the sound of human voices. As it became later, my fears increased in proportion. I grew too superstitious and nervous to keep the door open. I not only closed it, but dragged a heavy box in front, for bolt there was none. Several ill-looking men had, during the day, asked their way to Toronto. I felt alarmed, lest such rude wayfarers should come tonight and demand a lodging, and find me alone and unprotected. Once I thought of running across to Mrs. Joe, and asking her to let one of the girls stay with me until Moodie returned, but the way in which I had been repulsed in the evening prevented me from making a second appeal to their charity.

Hour after hour wore away, and the crowing of the cocks proclaimed midnight, and yet they came not. I had burnt out all my wood, and I dared not open the door to fetch in more. The candle was expiring in the socket, and I had not courage to go up into the loft and procure another before it went finally out. Cold, heart-weary, and faint, I sat and cried. Every now and then the furious barking of the dogs at the neighbouring farms, and the loud cackling of the geese upon our own, made me hope that they were coming; and then I listened till the beating of my own heart excluded all other sounds. Oh, that unwearied brook! how it sobbed and moaned like a fretful child;—what unreal terrors and fanciful illusions my too active mind conjured up, whilst listening to its mysterious tones!

Just as the moon rose, the howling of a pack of wolves, from the great swamp in our rear, filled the whole air. Their yells were answered by the barking of all the dogs in the vicinity, and the geese, unwilling to be behind-hand in the general confusion, set up the most discordant screams. I had often heard, and even been amused, during the winter, particularly on thaw nights, with hearing the howls of these formidable wild beasts, but I had never before heard them alone, and when one dear to me was abroad amid their haunts. They were directly in the track that Moodie and Monaghan must have taken; and I now made no doubt that they had been attacked and killed on their return through the woods with the cow, and I wept and sobbed until the cold grey dawn peered in upon me through the small dim window. I have passed many a long cheerless night, when my dear husband was away from me during the rebellion, and I was left in my forest home with five little children, and only an old Irish woman to draw and cut wood for my fire, and attend to the wants of the family, but that was the saddest and longest night I ever remember.

Just as the day broke, my friends the wolves set up a parting benediction, so loud, and wild, and near to the house, that I was afraid lest they should break through the frail window, or come down the low, wide chimney, and rob me of my child. But their detestable howls died away in the distance, and the bright sun rose up and dispersed the wild horrors of the night, and I looked once more timidly around me. The sight of the table spread, and the uneaten supper, renewed my grief, for I could not divest myself of the idea that Moodie was dead. I opened the door, and stepped forth into the pure air of the early day. A solemn and beautiful repose still hung like a veil over the face of Nature. The mists of night still rested upon the majestic woods, and not a sound but the flowing of the waters went up in the vast stillness. The earth had not yet raised her matin hymn to the throne of the Creator. Sad at heart, and weary and worn in spirit, I went down to the spring and washed my face and head, and drank a deep draught of its icy waters. On returning to the house, I met, near the door, old Brian the hunter, with a large fox dangling across his shoulder, and the dogs following at his heels.

"Why! Mrs. Moodie, what is the matter? You are early abroad this morning, and look dreadful ill. Is anything wrong at home? Is the baby or your husband sick?"

"Oh!" I cried, bursting into tears, "I fear he is killed by the wolves."

The man stared at me, as if he doubted the evidence of his senses, and well he might; but this one idea had taken such strong possession of my mind that I could admit no other. I then told him, as well as I could find words, the cause of my alarm, to which he listened very kindly and patiently.

"Set your heart at rest; your husband is safe. It is a long journey on foot to Mollineux, to one unacquainted with a blazed path in a bush road. They have stayed all night at the black man's shanty, and you will see them back at noon."

I shook my head and continued to weep.

"Well, now, in order to satisfy you, I will saddle my mare, and ride over to the nigger's, and bring you word as fast as I can."

I thanked him sincerely for his kindness, and returned, in somewhat better spirits, to the house. At ten o'clock my good messenger returned with the glad tidings that all was well.

The day before, when half the journey had been accomplished, John Monaghan let go the rope by which he led the cow, and she had broken away through the woods, and returned to her old master; and when they again reached his place, night had set in, and they were obliged to wait until the return of day. Moodie laughed heartily at all my fears; but indeed I found them no joke.

—

When our resolution was formed to sell our farm, and take up our grant of land in the backwoods, no one was so earnest in trying to persuade us to give up this ruinous scheme as our friend Brian B——, who became quite eloquent in his description of the trials and sorrows that awaited us. During the last week of our stay in the township of H——, he visited us every evening, and never bade us good-night without a tear moistening his cheek. We parted with the hunter as with an old friend; and we never met again. His fate was a sad one. After we left that part of the country, he fell into a moping melancholy, which ended in self-destruction. But a kinder or warmer-hearted man, while he enjoyed the light of reason, has seldom crossed our path.

Excerpted from the New Canadian Library edition of
Roughing It in the Bush; or, Life in Canada *by Susanna*
Moodie, published by McClelland & Stewart in 1989.

Author Biography: Moodie's Literary Life

Now that you have read the excerpt from Susanna Moodie and have some sense of the historical context in which she wrote, your group may very well desire a more specific understanding of Moodie the person and Moodie the writer.

Susanna Moodie, née Strickland, was born near Bungay, Suffolk, in England in 1803 into a literary family. She had two brothers and five sisters, four of whom became writers, including Catharine Parr Traill, best known for *The Backwoods of Canada: Being Letters from the Wife of an Emigrant Officer, Illustrative of the Domestic Economy of British America,* and Eliza and Agnes, co-authors of *Lives of the Queens of England.* Susanna's first published work, *Spartacus: A Roman Story,* appeared when she was nineteen.

In 1831 she moved to London, where she became involved with the anti-slavery movement and met her future husband, John Dunbar Moodie. The Moodies and their first child emigrated to Canada in 1832 and settled near Cobourg, in what is now Ontario. They spent two difficult years there trying to make a living as bush farmers. In 1834 they moved to Douro Township so that they could be closer to her sister, Catharine, and her brother Samuel

Strickland, who had by that time established himself as one the area's most successful foreign settlers. In 1837, because of the Rebellion, Moodie's husband was recalled to active service and the family finally obtained a measure of financial security. In 1839, the Moodies moved to Belleville, after Dunbar Moodie was appointed sheriff of Victoria District (later called Hastings County).

From 1839 to 1851 Moodie published poems and prose in various magazines and in 1852 she published *Roughing It in the Bush; or, Life in Canada*. The following year she published the sequel, *Life in the Clearings versus the Bush*.

She lived in Belleville until 1869, when her husband died. After his death, she lived primarily in Toronto until her death in 1885. In her final years she wrote very little, although she did spend more of her time painting.

Apart from the works for which she is best known, she also wrote five works of fiction, eight works of fiction for young readers, and two collections of poetry, together with various anti-slavery tracts, including *Negro Slavery Described by a Negro: Being the Narrative of Ashton Warner, a Native of St. Vincent's*.

Whether or not this information leads to an inspired book club conversation, your fellow group members will find it important and helpful, and this kind of information is especially relevant when you are discussing personal memoirs, since you can draw on it for subsequent, related discussion topics.

History in the Making: *Roughing It in the Bush* Within Its Historical Context

In certain respects, the experiences that Susanna Moodie relates in *Roughing It in the Bush* are as remote from our own lives as the ones in *Star Wars*. The idea of being plucked from genteel British society to live out in the harsh Canadian wilderness, plowing fields for the first time, learning how to make coffee from dandelions and not seeing the nearest neighbour throughout the entire winter season is a concept that we, luckily, do not have to entertain in our own lives, where our biggest complaint is about trudging down the block to buy a superior caffe latte.

But the idea of positioning the historical context of a non-fiction writer is more complex than simply discovering the years in which they wrote, the setting, the society around them. When discussing all writers, but particularly writers of non-fiction, your group has to work together to understand why the writer wanted to write about this subject, and how that "why" has informed the nature of the book they have produced.

In the case of a well-known writer like Moodie, the why is something that can be found with a few minutes of research on the Internet, in library reference guides or in the "Introductions" or "Afterwords" to any decent edition of her work. In discussing the historical context of any work of non-fiction, one of the first questions that your book club group should ask is, quite simply, why was the author writing. According to her own account, Moodie is writing to share her story of a particularly miserable deception. Her memoirs, then, are not simply an account of her experiences; they are a warning to all those who were also entertaining the possibility of following in her footsteps. She is not simply saying, "I endured hardships"; she is saying, "I endured hardships because I was deceived, and I want you to read this book so that you won't be deceived in the same way."

Both Moodie and her sister Catharine Parr Traill came to Canada under very specific circumstances. As Moodie herself tells us in her own "Introduction" to her book, she was a part of a major wave of British emigration to Canada around the early 1830s, when discharged British soldiers on half-pay were encouraged to take up land in Canada in order to sustain themselves and their families: "...a class perfectly unfitted by their previous habits and education for contending with the stern realities of emigrant life." The result of this general trend, according to Moodie, was great hardship for anyone who accepted the British government's offer, since the land-dealers who were found in Canada were waiting to take advantage of all unsuspecting victims: "Oh, ye dealers in wild lands—ye speculators in the folly and credulity of your fellow man—what a mass of misery, and of misrepresentation productive of that misery, have ye not to answer for!"

Understanding the historical context of the work and of the author's design in writing the work does a great deal to orient our discussion of the book itself. Considering the fact that Moodie was not writing her book to celebrate her experience, but rather to use those experiences to promote a specific agenda within a specific historical moment, we must look at her sketch of "Brian, the Still-Hunter" within this context. What are the qualities of this chapter that participate in Moodie's plan to dissuade potential settlers and to emphasize the hardship of her experiences? First, she makes certain that we see Brian as a woodsman with a noble spirit who, necessarily, endures a tragic life because of his choice to live his life in the backwoods of Canada: "His fate was a sad one. After we left that part of the country, he fell into a moping melancholy, which ended in self-destruction. But a kinder or warmer-hearted man, while he enjoyed the light of reason, has seldom crossed our path."

In instances like this, knowing the historical context of the book as a whole does a great deal to enhance the quality of the discussion your group can have. Whenever your group reads a work of non-fiction, you must be aware that the writer has an infinite number of choices about the subject material. In reading a biography or memoirs, what is interesting is not simply the fact that the writer has chosen to express these hundred or two hundred incidents to create the story of a life, but that he or she has omitted an infinite number of other anecdotes and incidents that didn't quite fit into that particular version of the story.

In the case of "Brian, the Still-Hunter," members of the group could ask questions such as: Of all the interesting experiences that Moodie must have had during her years in the backwoods, why did she choose to write about this one? What are the unique qualities of this character, of this story, that fit so well into the version of the story that she is trying to tell?

There are various answers to these questions, each of which can lead to very meaningful discussions. Certainly, Brian is important to Moodie because he clearly fits into the message she is trying to communicate: in this setting, even the finest person will ultimately fall to madness and ruin. Some critics have even suggested that the experience of the backwoods of Canada drove Moodie herself half-crazy. This may be another reason why she feels such an intense kinship with Brian.

Depending on the commitment of the group to the book, an idea like this could be taken even further. One of the recurring ideas throughout *Roughing It in the Bush* is that Moodie is both attracted to and terrified by the sublime quality of the natural setting around her: "Oh, that unwearied brook! how it sobbed and moaned like a fretful child;—what unreal terrors and fanciful illusions my too active mind conjured up, whilst listening to its mysterious tones!" Clearly, Moodie is captivated by the double quality of nature, the beauty and the chaos, the majesty and the danger, what Margaret Atwood has called Moodie's "violent duality," or the "inescapable doubleness of her own vision." This again participates in the context of the work, in that she is trying to communicate that, in Canada, there may be great beauty in the surroundings, but there are also always great perils lurking within that beauty. It is not difficult to see why Brian, the Still-Hunter, as a character who is both at one with nature and ultimately destroyed by it, would be a figure about whom Moodie would be very much interested.

There are numerous other questions that your group might ask in discussing the historical context of a work, each of which can guide you toward equally meaningful insights. If your group knows anything about various historical literary periods, you might want to think about what Moodie's own literary influences may have been. Once again, this information is readily available in various reference sources. In this case, Moodie was predominantly influenced by the British Romantics, and her work, even within the specific messages that she is trying to communicate, has a distinctly Romantic quality to it. For example, the sense that Moodie is both spiritually elevated and terrified by the untamed wilderness around her is a distinctly Romantic concept. Whenever you are discussing any writer, you should try, if possible, to determine the influences that come into play, whether they are a historical trend or other writers.

As was the case in our discussion of Fitzgerald's *The Great Gatsby*, issues of social class also play a tremendous role in Moodie's non-fictional writing. In coming to Canada, Moodie was highly aware that she was of a different social caste than many of the other settlers and Americans whom she encountered. This made her feel both victimized and superior. In the case of Brian, the Still-Hunter, this is important, in that she first becomes interested in Brian as someone who seems to possess a sense of etiquette far above the other settlers that she finds around her, and this leads her into a search for his superior qualities.

Knowing Moodie's historical context enables the group better to understand and sympathize with her plight, her observations, the construction of her story and her contradictions. Although that might still not be enough. A friend of ours read *Roughing It* in her club a few years ago: "I liked it, but parts of it I still had real problems with—her classism, her racism, her pomposity, her colonial mentality. Sometimes this stuff just drove me and some other members of my group crazy."

As you have seen from this brief sampling, there are many different approaches that one can take to follow this discussion. Of course, you can choose the one best suited to your group. But it has been our experience that these discussions usually relate back to the members of the group and their own experiences: "You think Moodie had problems, you should have felt how cold my feet were this morning as I was walking to the bus..." If there is no other direction to take in understanding the context, you can always contrast the experience of the writer with your own. Or at least that approach may work to get you started on a meaningful group discussion.

Stranger than Fiction: Symbolism, Writing Style and Voice of the Narrator

Susanna Moodie begins *Roughing It in the Bush* with the following epigraph:

> *I sketch from Nature, and the picture's true;*
> *Whate'er the subject, whether grave or gay,*
> *Painful experience in a distant land*
> *Made it mine own.*

Although *Roughing It* often has the look and feel of a factual account, and although it often seems that Moodie would like us to believe it is so, the book is as contrived and constructed as any work of fiction that your book club will read. We should remember that Moodie began her career as a novelist at an early age, and by the time she was nineteen she had already published her first novel. She fully understood the need to keep the reader engaged and knew how to craft her language in ways that engage, instruct and entertain her readers. As the critic Susan Glickman says in the afterword to this book, the characters and events Moodie relates are chosen "as much for their illustrative value as for their veracity. Thus, for example, we are given *three* fires, in ascending order of danger, and *three* failed gentleman-settlers....There is a certain symbolic neatness about such patterns of repetition that owes as much to literature as to life."

Whenever your book club is discussing a work of non-fiction, try, together, to pay attention to the signs that the writer is moulding the story in a particular way to generate a particular argument. Moodie is a perfect case of this, and in the following pages we show you how your group can treat non-fiction with a heightened critical eye.

Roughing It was not published just after it had been written, as might have been the case if it were a journalistic account of her time in this new land. In fact, it was not published in London until 1852, fifteen years after the stories and tribulations that it relates, and was not published in Canada until 1871. Moodie had plenty of time to recast, elaborate on and embroider the occurrences that she no doubt took notes on as they happened.

The chapter that we have quoted above is representative of the way Moodie reworks her material into a coherent and literary construction. She is constantly invoking her own memories, while desirous of writing as though things are happening to her at that instant. "O'er memory's glass I see this shadow flit" she says in the opening poem that begins the chapter, and then writes with short spare images, and specific actions, as though it is a contemporary account. Brian's first visit to her "old shanty" is sudden and not just a little disconcerting. His four words of instruction to his dogs are the only snippets of the first visit from this taciturn, rough-hewn fellow.

Over the course of the chapter he becomes much better known to us and to Moodie. From a person barely able to grunt he turns into a rather verbose philosopher of the woods, full of information about his thoughts on hunting, the beauty of nature and the many difficulties that the Moodies must be mindful of as they pursue their "ruinous scheme" of settling in Canada. Along the way we receive information about him from a variety of sources. Moodie tells us "I must find out who and what he is" and then proceeds to chart this passage of discovery for the reader. Much of the background on Brian comes from Layton, an old soldier and a much feared neighbour, whom Moodie quotes at great length. Either she has a sterling memory that can recall, verbatim, hundreds of words of dialogue at one go, or she is able to re-invent and form what was more than likely a meandering and elliptical conversation into a coherent whole.

The chapter builds to a tragic crescendo of Moodie's emotional attachment to Brian and his eventual "self-destruction." In twenty pages Moodie has taken us from seeing a "strange being" invading her privacy to a familiar man who has tears in his eyes every night he bids them adieu. This transformation is present for the reader because Moodie knows what to tell the reader and when to tell it. There is a careful pattern, a defined structure to the chapter, as there is to the overall book.

Another way to think about this chapter and the entire book is to ask yourself if the writing of history or travel literature or even a memoir is a subjective or an objective occupation. Is it possible for two people who have seen the same bit of life—the birth of a child, a revolution or war, the death of a family member, the same disaster or celebration—to describe the scene in the same way? Of course not. Every person brings a distinct set of talents, personal baggage, insecurities and strengths that go into his or her observation and recording of that event or action.

From one perspective, Moodie had a very clear understanding of why she was writing. As she says in the chapter "Adieu to the Woods": "If these sketches should prove the means of deterring one family from sinking their property, and shipwrecking all their hopes, by going to reside in the backwoods of Canada, I shall consider myself amply repaid for revealing the secrets of the prison-house, and feel that I have not toiled and suffered in the wilderness in vain." All of what she writes in *Roughing It* is concerned, to one degree or another, with this didactic purpose. It is a sentiment that informs and colours everything that she writes. Yet is this the best way to tell a story, to relate factual or truthful information?

Even though she wanted to dissuade people from moving to Canada, there is a straddling of desires within her task, as is evident from the chapter quoted here. She comes to have sincere affection for Brian and the reader naturally follows her in this sentiment. It is up to us as readers to follow her through her story and assess how much trust we put into her story.

Of course, Moodie is not the only writer of supposed fact to depend upon fictional and rhetorical devices to tell us a story. Robertson Davies always did considerable research on, for example, the stage, or Jungian psychoanalysis before he sat down to write us a new novel. Michael Ondaatje recast the story of a Hungarian soldier for his novel *The English Patient* and reshaped the life of jazz musician Buddy Bolden for his earlier work *Coming Through Slaughter*. James Joyce's *Ulysses* is perhaps the most famous example of a fictionalized work based so completely on facts. The Dublin of 1904 is so carefully presented in this complicated novel that it has been said the book could function as an atlas of the city's streets. The American author Mary McCarthy also saw this reliance on facts in Leo Tolstoy. As she says, "You can learn how to make strawberry jam from *Anna Karenina*."

What the author does with the facts before him or her is what makes a work truly come alive for the reader, and is also what your book club should focus on in group discussion. Although we chose *Roughing It* as a representative and provocative work of non-fiction, the members of your book club should, in all your readings, give thought and discussion time to this issue of fact versus fiction, of how a writer crafts and shapes the material, of what makes a piece of writing "true" as opposed to merely based on fact.

Just the Facts, Ma'am: Theme and Character in *Roughing It in the Bush*

Discussing the "themes" of a work of non-fiction (especially a memoir) is a little trickier than doing so with a novel since, in theory, the writer of the work of non-fiction is not shaping the work into a good story in order to get a specific "message" across to the reader, but is merely presenting the facts. In theory, then, the person writing the work of non-fiction simply relates the events or the ideas as they really happened or as they really are, and if that creates an interesting or worthwhile read, then fine, but if not, then at least the truth has been told accurately.

This is not to say that the non-fiction writer is necessarily lying, but simply that he or she chooses from among the available material to take what is needed to tell that particular version of the story. In the case of "Brian, the Still-Hunter," Moodie was definitely crafting and shaping the story into the version to reflect the themes that she was trying to express. Moodie could certainly have given us a much different version of Brian if she were trying to express different themes. In her version, Brian is presented as a noble spirit driven toward self-destruction by his exposure to the wilderness. She emphasizes his gentlemanly characteristics, his good manners (in stark contrast to those of other characters in the book) and his good deeds.

When others speak poorly of him, she chooses not to give their version of the story, or their impression of him, as much validity as her own. For instance, when the character of Layton provides a version of Brian's suicidal episode and presents him to Moodie in a very poor light, Moodie uses language to dismiss this perception of Brian that runs counter to her own: "Layton departed, and left me brooding over the sad tale which he had told in such an absurd and jesting manner. It was evident from the account he had given of Brian's attempted suicide, that the hapless hunter was not wholly answerable for his conduct—that he was a harmless maniac."

In quoting Layton, Moodie re-creates Layton's poor use of English as yet another strategy in dismissing him: "The doctor came, and sewed up his throat; and his wife—poor crittur!—came to nurse him. Bad as he was, she was mortal fond of him!" But Layton does show us a great deal that Moodie, in her version, chooses to ignore, including his long-suffering wife, his violent behaviour and his drinking. Moodie includes Layton's version in her sketch to illustrate the general public perception of Brian that runs counter to her own, but in reading that other perception, your book club can recognize and discuss how there is more than one way to tell the same story in a work of non-fiction. In this case, Moodie gives us both her version and Layton's version. In her version, Brian is both a noble spirit and a "harmless maniac"; in Layton's version he is an abusive alcoholic and a potentially very harmful maniac.

As we know, Moodie's intention in writing *Roughing It in the Bush* was to show future potential settlers that the experience of settling in Canada is wrought with perils, dangers and hardships. Her themes, then, all relate in some way to this intent. In her version of Brian, she wants to show that even the finest gentleman, when exposed to the Canadian wilderness, will deteriorate. Moodie is happy to show us how kind Brian is to her child, Katie, but to expand upon his relationship with his own children, who are left lurking in the background of the sketch, would be to damage the perception of the gentle, giving soul that she wishes to give us in her sketch. To provide a broader picture of his life would be to challenge her own themes, and she must therefore pick through only those aspects of the story that support her version and sweep the rest under the rug.

When you are discussing a work of fiction, it is difficult to challenge the "message" or "theme" of the writer, since the story is a product of that person's imagination. But when it comes to non-fiction, it is always helpful to challenge the writer. If you are reading an "advice" book, you can always question the advice, since your take on the subject (building good relationships, getting ahead in the business world, healing your spirit, and so on) is usually as valid as that of the writer. And if you are reading accounts of actual events (history, biography, autobiography), then you can always be certain that the writer is telling you only the version he or she wants you to see, and that behind that version are countless others (call it the "Layton factor"), which are always suggested, challenging the author's own version.

Other Readings and Sources

If your club is particularly ambitious, some or all of you may be keen enough to seek out other works influenced by or involving the writer in question. Susanna Moodie has become a legendary figure in Canada for her remarkable powers of observation and her personal and sometimes idiosyncratic documentation of the harsh early years of settling this vast country. Among the other readings your club may choose to explore are the writings of her sister, Catharine Parr Traill, and her brother Samuel Strickland, author of *Twenty-Seven Years in Canada West*. In contrast to Moodie's despair, Traill's work is notable for its optimism and faith in God. At one point in *Roughing It*, Moodie refers to her sister's more positive vision of living in the bush: "My conversations with her had quite altered the aspect of the country, and predisposed me to view things in the most favourable light."

Margaret Atwood is the most notable of contemporary writers who have been influenced by Moodie. Her collection of poems *The Journals of Susanna Moodie* is a poetical reconstruction of various Moodie sketches and includes a poem entitled "Dream 2: Brian the Still Hunter," in which Moodie, or perhaps Brian, or perhaps Atwood herself, asks: "Is God just to his creatures?"

For Atwood, Moodie continues to haunt our collective understanding of the country. The final poem in the collection has Moodie riding a bus along St. Clair Avenue in contemporary downtown Toronto: "I am the old woman / sitting across from you on the bus, / her shoulders drawn up like a shawl."

Other contemporary authors who have used Moodie as a character or a voice in their works include Robertson Davies in his book *At My Heart's Core*, Carol Shields in *Small Ceremonies* and Elizabeth Hopkins in her one-woman play *Susanna*.

Among the other works you may choose to read alongside Moodie's is Northrop Frye's *The Bush Garden: Essays on the Canadian Imagination*. Frye believes that Canadians respond to nature with "deep terror" and that we live in a garrison culture, where we set up civilized structures to help us cope with the dangerous and threatening world of nature.

If you are interested in more biographical detail you might choose to read *Gentle Pioneers: Five Nineteenth-Century Canadians*, by Audrey Morris or "The Strickland Sisters" in Clara Thomas's book *The Clear Spirit: Twenty Canadian Women and Their Times*.

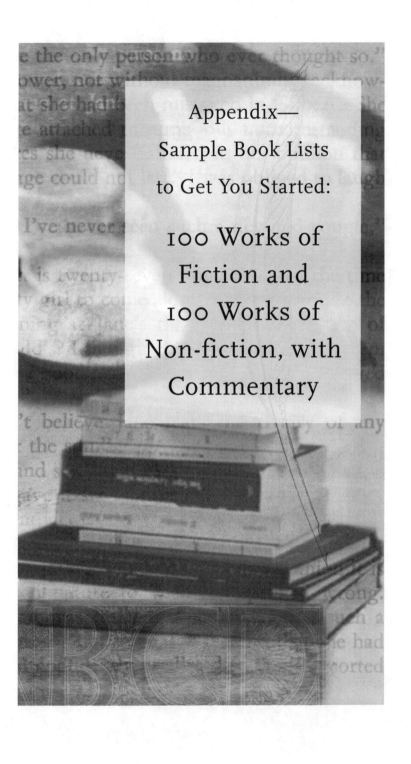

Appendix—
Sample Book Lists
to Get You Started:

100 Works of
Fiction and
100 Works of
Non-fiction, with
Commentary

Polonius: *What do you read, my Lord?*
Hamlet: *Words, words, words.*

SHAKESPEARE

These lists—arranged alphabetically by book title—are, by
definition, incomplete. Many of the books that you or your book
club love, or that are good "book club books," are not included
here because of space limitations. We also have our own idiosyncratic reasons for including some of the titles that follow. There
are, of course, a limitless number of other excellent, challenging,
provocative books for your book club to explore and enjoy,
including plays and collections of poems, that we have not even
attempted to list here.

Use these lists as an introductory guide, and make sure that
you also seek out other sources of book titles that will bring
your club alive, including your own reading, the Internet, best-
seller lists from various publications, your local library and
bookstores both large and small. Happy searching and happy
reading!

Fiction

THE ADVENTURES OF HUCKLEBERRY FINN, by MARK TWAIN.
Don't let your book group be fooled into thinking that this is just
for children or teens. If you haven't read it lately, you will be surprised at how many challenging and troubling issues are raised
by Twain in this classic novel.

ALIAS GRACE, by MARGARET ATWOOD. The richly acclaimed
Atwood is always provocative and engaging. Here she reclaims
the story of Grace Marks, a nineteenth-century maid accused of
killing her employer and his mistress. There's much here and in
Atwood's other books to keep your group talking and speculating.

AS FOR ME AND MY HOUSE, by SINCLAIR ROSS. A preacher's
wife struggles through the Great Depression on the Canadian
prairie. The perfect novel for any group that wants to examine the
reliability of the narrator in fictional works.

AS I LAY DYING, by WILLIAM FAULKNER. If you pick up one of
Faulkner's difficult works first, you may be scared off and never
want to read him again. Start with this novel, which is at once
dark, troubling and very, very funny.

AS WE ARE NOW, by MAY SARTON. A powerful novel narrated by
a woman stuck away in an old age home. The ending will stay
with you long after you close the book. The members of your
group may never look at the aged again in quite the same light.

THE AWAKENING, by KATE CHOPIN. This early feminist classic
of a New Orleans woman rejecting her social role and discovering
her true identity at the turn of the century will enable your fellow
group members to reflect on persisting gender roles today.

BEAUTIFUL LOSERS, by LEONARD COHEN. Read about Canadian political radicals, the last member of a dying native tribe, hardcore sexual experimentation...and then turn to the second chapter! This novel, written from the heart of the '60s, is not for the faint of heart.

THE BEAUTIFUL ROOM IS EMPTY, by EDMUND WHITE. One of America's best-known gay novelists, White writes about male homosexuality and the impact of AIDS on our communities. Your group will find this and his other fiction and non-fiction important documents on social history.

THE BELL JAR, by SYLVIA PLATH. One month after the publication of this book, her only novel, Plath committed suicide. It is a powerful, harrowing account of a woman's mental breakdown. Your group may want to read a few poems by Plath together with this book, although they too are profoundly disturbing.

BELOVED, by TONI MORRISON. America's violent racist past literally comes back to haunt a family of escaped slaves. This is not an easy book, and your group members should be prepared to be deeply disturbed by Morrison's story. But it is also well worth the effort, as is the excellent film version.

BILLY BATHGATE, by E. L. DOCTOROW. An adolescent boy becomes entrapped in a story of mob life and learns some valuable lessons in the process. A good light read for a book club just starting out.

CALL IT SLEEP, by HENRY ROTH. Written at the height of the Great Depression, this novel slept for decades before Roth was rediscovered by literary critics in the 1960s. A complex Freudian tale of an immigrant boy and his tyrannical father.

THE CANNIBAL GALAXY, by CYNTHIA OZICK. The perfect novel for any group of educators or any group of readers with children in the education system. A close and surprising look at how we educate and how we assess our children's potential.

THE CATCHER IN THE RYE, by J. D. SALINGER. This novel on the disaffection of youth and the desire to find honesty amidst society's false fronts is without peer. It can be read again and again. Your group may choose it precisely because everyone may have read it long ago and wants a fresh look at it.

CATCH 22, by JOSEPH HELLER. Perhaps the funniest American novel ever written. Your group will laugh aloud together discussing the antics of these American soldiers and their efforts to escape their many predicaments.

THE COLLECTED STORIES OF MAVIS GALLANT. Gallant is a master of the short story, as these fifty-two stories attest. Your group will find much to ponder in these richly layered stories, including how precarious our lives often are and how much it takes to survive.

THE COLOR PURPLE, by ALICE WALKER. An epistolary novel that brings out the unique language and hardships of African American life in the South. Some in your group may find Walker's language difficult, while others will argue that it's well worth the effort.

THE CONSERVATIONIST, by NADINE GORDIMER. Much of Gordimer's writing is concerned with the alienation and racism present in her native South Africa. Your group may want to choose this book as an entrance into her other novels and short stories.

CRACKPOT, by ADELE WISEMAN. A darkly humorous story of an immigrant prostitute with a heart of gold who painstakingly develops her own mythology from her parents' stories of the old world. This book contains a profound understanding of those who live on the margins of society.

DAISY MILLER, by HENRY JAMES. Everyone should read some James at some point in life, but most of his work is just too demanding to pick up at the end of a busy day. *Daisy Miller* is his most readable, accessible work, and it will give you a glimpse into all of James's major themes.

DEAD SOULS, by NIKOLAI GOGOL. One of the great literary satires, this book follows the adventures of Chichikov, a dismissed civil servant in search of fortune. Your group will find it charming and comic but with a moral tone. Gogol burned the second volume, so the book remains unfinished, a fact that is worthy of discussion.

DEATH IN VENICE, by THOMAS MANN. Your group will find this a masterful novella of longing, the quest for beauty and the role of the artist in society. The excellent movie starring Dirk Bogarde is a fitting complement to the complexity of the novel.

THE DEATH OF ARTEMIO CRUZ, by CARLOS FUENTES. Mexican novelist, critic and diplomat, Fuentes is an intelligent and imaginative writer. *Artemio Cruz* is about a despicable individual who has achieved his wealth through corruption and ruthlessness. Your group may discuss elements of Mexico's history woven throughout the story.

THE ENGLISH PATIENT, by MICHAEL ONDAATJE. You've seen the movie, now try the book. Ondaatje's richly textured and lyrical prose will hypnotize some members of your group although it may alienate others. You may also complement your reading of this novel with a sampling of Ondaatje's poetry.

FALL ON YOUR KNEES, by ANN-MARIE MACDONALD. A vivid and compelling multi-generational saga about an immigrant family in Cape Breton. A complex novel, reminiscent of Dickens. For any group looking for a challenging read.

FIFTH BUSINESS, by ROBERTSON DAVIES. Throughout his many books Davies is wise, witty and always engaging. Your group can read *Fifth Business* as a fascinating biography of Dunstan Ramsay, as a Jungian novel or as a mythic tale of saints and the devil. Don't overlook the next two novels in this trilogy, *The Manticore* and *World of Wonders*.

THE FIXER, by BERNARD MALAMUD. An ordinary man is falsely accused of a crime and discovers his own insight, intelligence and heroism. Though there is not much action in this novel, your group will be amazed at how gripping it remains throughout.

THE GHOST ROAD, by PAT BARKER. This book has quickly become a classic of First World War literature. A skilful blending of fact and fiction, *The Ghost Road* is at times bleak and at other times humorous and at other times frighteningly realistic. It's part three of a trilogy but your group can read it on its own.

THE GOD OF SMALL THINGS, by ARUNDHATI ROY. The abundantly talented Roy says she may never write another novel, so if your group wants to read the entire oeuvre of an author, start here. It's the recent history of India seen through the eyes of twins and it is a charming, inventive and sumptuous read.

A GOOD MAN IS HARD TO FIND, by FLANNERY O'CONNOR. The short stories collected in this volume helped establish O'Connor's reputation as a master of the form. They are poetic and deal with justice, morality and redemption. One or two stories per meeting is plenty.

THE GRAPES OF WRATH, by JOHN STEINBECK. An impoverished family of farmers seeks greener pastures in California but finds only deeper sorrow. Try *Of Mice and Men* if you are committed to reading Steinbeck but are looking for something shorter.

GREAT EXPECTATIONS, by CHARLES DICKENS. The famous story of a young Victorian man who becomes tangled in complex plots of romance, wealth and disappointment. An excellent selection for groups whose members have never read Dickens but always wanted to.

THE HEART IS A LONELY HUNTER, by CARSON McCULLERS. McCullers said that the central theme of all her writing is "spiritual isolation." This is a brilliant, unsettling novel about a deaf-mute in a Georgia mill town. Not for groups looking for sweet and light reading.

HEART OF DARKNESS, by JOSEPH CONRAD. A classic novella of a journey into the horror of the human spirit. You may never visit the Belgian Congo but this book will teach you things you dimly know about the ways of the heart and the ways of the soul. A subsequent viewing of Francis Ford Coppola's *Apocalypse Now* will complement your reading nicely.

HIGH FIDELITY, by NICK HORNBY. Romance through the eyes of a thirty-something male adolescent. The men in your group will laugh nervously, the women will laugh bitterly and the accusations will be traded freely.

THE HOUSE OF SLEEP, by JONATHAN COE. An intelligent and invigorating novel about sleep and its dreamy and sometimes nightmarish entanglements. One of those novels that cannot be discussed until all members of your group have read the entire book.

THE HOUSE OF THE SPIRITS, by ISABEL ALLENDE. A powerful and poetic novel in the magic realist tradition. Allende combines in a seamless whole the political realities of Latin America and the day-to-day realities of ordinary citizens.

HUMBOLDT'S GIFT, by SAUL BELLOW. This thinly disguised rendition of Bellow's friendship with poet Delmore Schwartz is intriguing for groups that like stories of complex literary lives. Book clubs looking for a shorter book can try Bellow's *Dangling Man* or *Seize the Day*.

HUNGER, by KNUT HAMSUN. The Nobel Prize winner's first novel. This book, about an aspiring writer, has had a profound influence on many contemporary writers. It may very well lead your group to read more of Hamsun's haunting, impulsive work.

IF MORNING EVER COMES, by ANNE TYLER. A series of events forces a young college student to come to terms with his own past. A good selection for any book club, but especially those composed of readers from 20 to 35 years old.

IF ON A WINTER'S NIGHT A TRAVELLER, by ITALO CALVINO. A complicated and sophisticated novel about the interplay of fiction and reality. If you're looking for literary theory and parody interwoven into the story, you'll find this non-linear book fascinating.

IN A FREE STATE, by V. S. NAIPAUL. This collection of stories may be the perfect introduction to Naipaul's unique way of looking at the relationship between colonizers and the colonized. Don't forget Naipaul's novels and non-fiction.

THE INVENTION OF THE WORLD, by JACK HODGINS. A magical, mysterious world populated by a cast of idiosyncratic, wonderful people. Your group will marvel at the sweep and the power of this energetic novel.

INVISIBLE MAN, by RALPH ELLISON. A disturbing and sometimes surreal novel of a young black man trying to survive in America. This novel will spark profound debates about different forms of oppression and bigotry among the members of any committed book club.

A LESSON BEFORE DYING, by ERNEST J. GAINES. A troubling novel of a black man condemned to execution in the American south, and a school teacher's efforts to give him back his humanity. This book also tackles the complex issue of our responsibility toward our home community.

THE LIVES OF GIRLS AND WOMEN, by ALICE MUNRO. A series of connected short stories about the artistic and sexual awakening of teenage girls. The perfect "Portrait of the Artist as a Young Person" for female and mixed groups.

LIVES OF THE SAINTS, by NINO RICCI. Ricci stormed onto the literary scene with this story of a woman exiled from her community in a small Italian village. It's the first book of a trilogy. Good for any group looking for a rich European flavour.

LOLITA, by VLADIMIR NABOKOV. Not to everyone's liking, this obsessive and disturbing book remains relevant and controversial. Your group should read the novel first and then may want to see either of the two movie versions.

THE LOVER, by MARGUERITE DURAS. A profoundly sensual and sexual novel of a young woman's love for a wealthy, dissolute older man. Duras spent her early years in Indochina and its hold on her imagination is skilfully re-created and enriched.

MADAME BOVARY, by GUSTAVE FLAUBERT. Known for his realism, Flaubert takes the story of a woman's adultery and treats it with sympathy and profound understanding. Savour this book and read it slowly—your group will not be disappointed.

MARTIN DRESSLER: THE TALE OF AN AMERICAN DREAMER, by STEVEN MILLHAUSER. A complex story of a young man who dreams of becoming one of New York City's great builders. Millhauser's prose style will disorient many readers, but the novel is sure to spark good debate.

MEDICINE RIVER, by THOMAS KING. A touching and funny novel of a native man's return to the community of his youth. King's accessible style makes this a good choice for any group wishing to discuss the treatment of native people in North America.

MEMOIRS OF HADRIAN, by MARGUERITE YOURCENAR. Yourcenar has somehow climbed into the mind of Hadrian, the second-century Roman emperor. If you let it, this book will lead into rich and rewarding contemplations on power, friendships and personal history.

MEMORY BOARD, by JANE RULE. A complex novel about family life, commitment and memory—its lapses, and the things we consciously choose to ignore. Like all Rule's work, the foundation of the story is the homosexual love between women. Full of humour and wisdom.

THE METAMORPHOSIS, by FRANZ KAFKA. One of the most memorable opening sentences in literature. This symbolic and disturbing novella is central to understanding modern literature. Kafka's short stories also are strange, curious and worth reading.

MIDDLEMARCH, by GEORGE ELIOT. This wonderful, long novel of romance and politics in nineteenth-century England is the perfect choice for reading over a long summer break. But don't be the only member of your group who doesn't know Eliot is a woman.

MIDNIGHT'S CHILDREN, by SALMAN RUSHDIE. This allegory about modern India is a good place for your group to begin reading Rushdie. Later you may want to tackle *The Satanic Verses*, a much more difficult read.

MOBY DICK, by HERMAN MELVILLE. Another one of those books that is far too long and challenging for a monthly book club meeting. Assign this one over a long break, and don't ignore the more scientific chapters in search of the plot.

MONEY, by MARTIN AMIS. Although all of Amis's best work examines sex, violence, greed and the disturbing underside of American culture, *Money* is Amis at his most wicked, most sinister and most funny. Take him with a pound of salt.

MY ÁNTONIA, by WILLA CATHER. A novel that pays tribute to the courage of immigrant settlers of America's frontier. Cather is a compassionate writer and your group will find this and her other novels to be both hard-nosed and uplifting.

THE NAME OF THE ROSE, by UMBERTO ECO. A brainy murder mystery set in a monastery. The success of this book surprised many, perhaps no one as much as the author himself, an Italian critic and semiotician. Lots of fun and the film is also well worth a viewing.

NINETEEN EIGHTY-FOUR, by GEORGE ORWELL. A brilliant essayist and journalist, Orwell wrote this book as a warning against totalitarianism. "Big Brother" and "Newspeak" were both coined here. Your group should not ignore his other works, especially the essay collections.

OBASAN, by JOY KOGAWA. A brutal, touching novel about the evacuation of the Japanese from the west coast of Canada during the Second World War. Kogawa's message is understated but your group will leave this book with new insights into the human condition.

ONE HUNDRED YEARS OF SOLITUDE, by GABRIEL GARCÍA MÁRQUEZ. A masterpiece of imagination and storytelling. Spans Latin-America from the 1820s to the 1920s. Don't let your club rush too quickly through it.

ONE TRUE THING, by ANNA QUINDLEN. A family crisis forces a strong-willed young woman to see the familiar New England setting of her past with fresh eyes. A sure favourite with female readers.

ON THE ROAD, by JACK KEROUAC. Still the defining classic of the American beatnik counter-culture of the 1950s and 1960s. Kerouac's tale about the American romance of the road is straight out of the tradition of Walt Whitman, and it inspired a generation to wander and explore the great frontier. Try to find some of the great recordings of Kerouac reading from his work.

THE OPTIMIST'S DAUGHTER, by EUDORA WELTY. Most of Welty's writing concerns small-town Mississippi life. Her handling of human relationships and the virtues that lie just beneath the surface—here she explores the bond between child and parent—may very well lead you to her other books.

A Passage to India, by E. M. Forster. A poignant look at the relationship between British and Indian cultures in the dying days of imperialism. Forster, a brilliant novelist and social critic, never goes out of style.

A Perfect Spy, by John Le Carré. Is your book club looking for a little mystery, a little international intrigue and a little psychological complexity? Then *A Perfect Spy* is the perfect novel. Le Carré is the standard against which all other mystery writers should be judged, and this is one of his most controlled works.

Portnoy's Complaint, by Philip Roth. Any book club that doesn't mind reading a novel that opens with several chapters about masturbation will have a great time with this psycho-analytical tirade on the search for the Jewish American identity.

A Portrait of the Artist as a Young Man, by James Joyce. Joyce produced only classics. This novel portrays the early years of Stephen Dedalus in rich and complex stream-of-consciousness form. A good preparation for any group wanting to tackle Joyce's *Ulysses*.

Possession, by A. S. Byatt. A true intellectual page-turner. It's the story of love, literary research and obsession, all wrapped up in the search for a mysterious woman. For any group wanting to explore the world of scholarly research, which is certainly not a dry undertaking in Byatt's hands.

Pride and Prejudice, by Jane Austen. Austen revolutionized the novel form by writing about ordinary people and their every-day struggles. With this and her other well-known works, your group could spend a whole season only on Austen.

THE RAZOR'S EDGE, by W. SOMERSET MAUGHAM. A perennial favourite about a young man who rejects American materialism and goes in search of meaning. This one will have even the most cynical group members questioning the values of their own lives.

REMAINS OF THE DAY, by KAZUO ISHIGURO. A diffident, aging butler is witness to complicated political manoeuvring during the Second World War. The story is subtle and fascinating and your group will find that Ishiguro's writing complements the movement of the novel.

ST. URBAIN'S HORSEMAN, by MORDECAI RICHLER. In the aftermath of the Holocaust, a Canadian filmmaker searches for answers and imagines a distant cousin as the world's Jewish avenging angel. Funny, poignant, bitterly satirical, it will have your club struggling for answers on how we can survive in a world where such atrocities are possible.

THE SCARLET LETTER, by NATHANIEL HAWTHORNE. Perhaps the most remarkable aspect of this novel about an outcast woman in Puritan society is how contemporary and relevant it seems to each subsequent generation. But whatever you do, don't rent the movie!

THE SECOND SCROLL, by A. M. KLEIN. A Canadian editor, on a mission to find new Israeli poetry, searches through Europe, Morocco and Israel for his uncle who has survived the Holocaust. The perfect read for a group looking for a very short, very complex novel.

SEE JANE RUN, by JOY FIELDING. Fielding writes psychological thrillers about ordinary women trapped in harrowing situations. She remains wildly popular internationally but is underappreciated here at home in Canada. A break from some of the more challenging works suggested elsewhere in these lists.

SHAKESPEARE'S DOG, by LEON ROOKE. A short, quirky and energetic novel, narrated by the Bard's dog, Hooker. Lusty and extravagant language. Perfect complement to any Shakespeare your club is reading.

THE SHIPPING NEWS, by E. ANNIE PROULX. Some in your group may have trouble absorbing Proulx's language, but it's well worth the struggle. Fishermen's knots, newspapers, an American family moving to Eastern Canada to start over again: everything Proulx writes about becomes lyrical and evocative.

THE STONE ANGEL, by MARGARET LAURENCE. Hagar Shipley is a central icon of Canadian literature. The novel travels back and forth through time and is both compassionate and defiant. Your group will quickly see why this novel is so well respected.

THE STONE DIARIES, by CAROL SHIELDS. An ordinary tale of an ordinary woman takes on mythic proportions when the details of her life are examined closely enough. This novel will give all members of your group new insight into the profound significance of their daily lives.

SUCH A LONG JOURNEY, by ROHINTON MISTRY. The most surprising aspect of this novel of a son's rebellion against his father in India is that it is written from the father's point of view. A great and sensitive story of generational and cultural clashes.

A SUITABLE BOY, by VIKRAM SETH. Weighing in at 1,349 pages, this may not be the best choice for your group if it insists on reading one book every two weeks. The prodigiously intelligent Seth depicts here the relations among four Indian families. His poetry and verse novel *The Golden Gate* are challenging but also worth a serious look.

THE SUN ALSO RISES, by ERNEST HEMINGWAY. Ever wonder what that lost generation of American expatriates was up to in Paris in the 1920s? Hemingway's classic novel will give your group a clear and disturbing depiction of the spirit of the age, something like *The Great Gatsby*'s European cousin.

SUNSHINE SKETCHES OF A LITTLE TOWN, by STEPHEN LEACOCK. This hilarious satire on small-town attitudes remains popular, and deservedly so. In discussing this book, your group can debate how innocent and quaint these characters and their town really are.

A THOUSAND ACRES, by JANE SMILEY. Shakespeare's *King Lear* gets replayed in the American heartland. This book probes the deep complexities of family relationships and may very well lead your group to read Smiley's other works.

TO KILL A MOCKINGBIRD, by HARPER LEE. You won't find a single reference to Gregory Peck in the novel, but you will find one of the most accessible, readable and enduring stories ever written on the subject of racism in America.

TO THE LIGHTHOUSE, by VIRGINIA WOOLF. A distinguished critic and novelist, Woolf experimented with the stream-of-consciousness form in this book. It's the stylized story of the poetical Mrs. Ramsay and the rational Mr. Ramsay and the contrasts between the female and the male ways of seeing the world.

ULYSSES, by JAMES JOYCE. A monumental work in every sense of the word. Savour the words and read the book slowly—one chapter per meeting is about right. This is not for any but the most dedicated book club. There is no shame in using one of the several *Ulysses* guidebooks on the market.

THE UNBEARABLE LIGHTNESS OF BEING, by MILAN KUNDERA. Set against the political upheaval of Czechoslovakia of the 1960s, this novel traces the sexual and political sympathies of a young doctor. The movie adaptation was good but still can't stand up to the power of Kundera's writing.

UNCLE TOM'S CABIN, by HARRIET BEECHER STOWE. This novel was a driving force in the abolition of slavery in the U.S. as well as the best seller of the nineteenth century. And yet your group may find it as problematic in its depiction of its slave characters as it is well intentioned.

UNDER THE VOLCANO, by MALCOLM LOWRY. An alcoholic British official tries to rebuild his life in Mexico. Perfect for any group that enjoys Mexico, drinking, stream-of-consciousness narratives or great reading.

THE WARS, by TIMOTHY FINDLEY. Within the insanity of the Second World War, an act of madness may be the only sane response. This novel will force your group to examine the question of how we look at history.

WHALE MUSIC, by PAUL QUARRINGTON. A proven favourite. Lots of laughs and just enough similarity to real rock and roll celebrities to keep the members of your group guessing and debating.

WHITE NOISE, by DON DELILLO. Delillo's greatest talent is in looking at ordinary America and seeing dark undercurrents at work. That, and a group of university professors specializing in Hitler studies, makes this novel irresistible.

WIDE SARGASSO SEA, by JEAN RHYS. West Indian Jean Rhys takes her influence from Charlotte Brontë's novel *Jane Eyre*, and all lovers of that book will find much to intrigue them here. Trapped in a loveless marriage, Antoinette Mason (Bertha in *Jane Eyre*) is confined to an attic and, well, you know what that can do to a person.

WOMEN OF SAND AND MYRRH, by HANAN AL-SHAYKH. Lebanese-born al-Shaykh is one of the few Arab women to publish internationally. This novel, about four women who are "treated to every luxury but freedom," uses simple language to tell profoundly courageous stories.

THE WORLD ACCORDING TO GARP, by JOHN IRVING. This story of mother and son emerging together as writers will keep your group engaged with its unexpected twists and turns. Probably the most universally appealing of Irving's many great novels.

Non-fiction

AMUSING OURSELVES TO DEATH, by NEIL POSTMAN. Think you and the members of your group understand about television and its influence? This is a persuasive wake-up call on the ways that TV shapes and limits our imagination.

ANGELA'S ASHES, by FRANK MCCOURT. A remarkable, tough memoir about a "miserable Irish Catholic childhood." A grand story in a rich tradition, full of drinking, coping with severe poverty and all the while revolving around the importance of storytelling.

ARCTIC DREAMS, by BARRY LOPEZ. This book is subtitled "Imagination and Desire in a Northern Landscape" and it is a brilliant account of Lopez's travels across the frozen North. For groups looking for natural history and inspired environmental writing.

ART AND ARDOR, by CYNTHIA OZICK. Ozick is one of America's most interesting novelists, and she is also a captivating theorist on the creative process. The essays included in this book would help the members of any book club develop their ability to read fiction critically and with keen insight.

ASSEMBLING CALIFORNIA, by JOHN MCPHEE. McPhee has tackled various topics, from the orange juice industry to nuclear terrorism. Here he writes with his typical engaging eloquence about plate tectonics. Your group may very well be convinced to read his other books after reading this fascinating account.

THE AUTOBIOGRAPHY, by BENJAMIN FRANKLIN. Before you start reading Donald Trump or Lee Iacocca spout off about their success, make sure that you know where the tradition of the "self-made man" biography began in America. Franklin is still one of the most fascinating individuals who ever lived, and you will certainly find much to debate.

BACKLASH, by SUSAN FALUDI. Faludi's major argument is that feminism was under attack by the establishment long before it was ever allowed to get off the ground. Now, a few years after her book was published, book club members can question how well her thesis holds up.

THE BACKWOODS OF CANADA, by CATHARINE PARR TRAILL. Sometimes referred to as Susanna Moodie's nicer sister, Traill takes her experiences as a Canadian settler much more in stride than Susanna, cataloguing the flora and fauna with a scientist's eye and always keeping her spirits high.

THE BEAUTY MYTH, by NAOMI WOLF. A damning study of dominant cultural trends that force women in our society to conform to strict and dangerous aesthetic codes. This book is guaranteed to open up some wounds and personal confessions, particularly among all-female or mixed groups.

BECOMING A MAN, by PAUL MONETTE. Monette died in 1995 of AIDS. He was 49. This remarkable memoir describes his life as a gay man, coping with his own demons and with the disease that was to kill him and many of his friends.

BETTER LIVING, by MARK KINGWELL. Kingwell has quickly become Canada's most important young political pundit. Some of this book, particularly the first half, will inspire some healthy banter on the importance of happiness in life.

BEYOND GOD THE FATHER: TOWARD A PHILOSOPHY OF WOMEN'S LIBERATION, by MARY DALY. Want some fireworks in your group? Daly has been called the first modern feminist philosopher and this book—convincing at parts, infuriating at others—will certainly encourage feisty debate.

BLOOD AND BELONGING: JOURNEYS INTO THE NEW NATIONALISM, by MICHAEL IGNATIEFF. Ignatieff is one of our most intelligent and compassionate thinkers. Here he takes us to various conflicts, including Québec, Northern Ireland and Serbia. His writing is full of wisdom about the folly of basing political decisions on ethnicity and race.

THE BOOK OF J, by HAROLD BLOOM. Bloom reprints one of the earliest versions of the Bible and then tries his hand at looking at it like a literary critic. Your group may want to begin by arguing whether this text challenges the divine origins of the more widely read, later version of the Bible.

THE BOOK OF THE COURTIER, by BALDESAR CASTIGLIONE. These days, everyone wants to sell you a book about getting ahead in the dog-eat-dog world of business. Why not have a look at how courtiers were charming kings and influencing dukes back in the Renaissance, and see how it compares to today? (Just replace "king" with "CEO" and "duke" with "VP.")

BOOM, BUST AND ECHO, by DAVID FOOT WITH DANIEL STOFF-MAN. One of the best-selling works of non-fiction in Canadian history, this book looks at demographic trends and tries to anticipate economic patterns. Your group may debate whether Foot is the next prophet, or whether this book is just common sense.

THE CANADIAN ESTABLISHMENT, by PETER C. NEWMAN. White guys with old money inherit and buy and sell this country again and again. For those who might like to feel connected to the lifestyles of the rich and Canadian, this book is still the Bible.

THE CATCHER WAS A SPY, by NICHOLAS DAWIDOFF. The fascinating story of an erudite major league baseball player who is recruited into becoming one of America's first nuclear era spies during the Second World War. If you are going to look at one sports biography, let this be the one.

CHUTZPAH, by ALAN M. DERSHOWITZ. The world's best-known celebrity lawyer and Harvard law professor comments on the formation of the American Jewish character. Any club will find it a provocative study of stereotypes.

CITY TO CITY, by JAN MORRIS. Travel writer Morris documents her adventures and observations from St. John's to Vancouver and north to Yellowknife. A joy to read, the book discusses how geography and culture shape the way we see ourselves.

THE CLOSING OF THE AMERICAN MIND, by ALLAN BLOOM. High-brow intellectual America goes mainstream. A brutally honest look at the failings and conservatism of the American higher education system. An important and challenging book for anyone close to university life, either as students, alumni or parents.

CONNECTING FLIGHTS, by ROBERT LEPAGE WITH RÉMY CHAREST. One of the world's greatest dramatists shares his views on how the creative process involves merging of elements from all cultures. This book is best for clubs whose members include some writers or artists.

COSMOS, by CARL SAGAN. A marvellous and engaging book that will get your group thinking about the vastness of our universe and the vastness of the imagination. Includes more than 250 full-colour illustrations.

THE CULT OF IMPOTENCE, by LINDA McQUAIG. This is not a book about sexual inadequacy. Always feisty and controversial, McQuaig destroys the myth that social programs must be dismantled if Canada is to compete globally. Your group may want to read this in concert with any publication from the Business Council on National Issues.

THE CULTURE OF COMPLAINT, by ROBERT HUGHES. Australian Hughes has become one of the most significant commentators on art today. Here he discusses how art has been co-opted to serve as therapy or as a tool in righting social wrongs or as political fodder. The writing is sometimes heady and theoretical but it's well worth the struggle.

THE DEATH AND LIFE OF GREAT AMERICAN CITIES, by JANE JACOBS. This is the most important book ever published on city planning. Jacobs argues that revitalizing old-fashioned houses and neighbourhoods is a much better way to go than dry, modernist planning.

DELMORE SCHWARTZ: THE STORY OF AN AMERICAN POET, by JAMES ATLAS. One of the few cases where the story of the artist's life is more interesting than the art itself. Schwartz is the classic tormented poet, connected to most major writers of his time, driven mad by personal demons. This book will captivate any group of modern poetry lovers.

THE DIARY OF A YOUNG GIRL, by ANNE FRANK. The famous found diary of a girl hiding in an Amsterdam attic before she perished in the Holocaust. Maybe the most accessible book for any group interested in learning about the twentieth century's darkest episode.

DOWN AND OUT IN PARIS AND LONDON, by GEORGE ORWELL. Prior to his rise to fame, the legendary novelist endured extreme poverty and misery. In this memoir of those years, he tells of how two countries respond differently to marginal vagrant culture.

AN EMPIRE OF THEIR OWN, by NEIL GABLER. It is possible that the first group of Hollywood moguls had a more profound impact on this century than any politician or philosopher. But what social forces created their vision of movie culture? This book takes you deep into their religious and personal histories.

ESSAYS, by MICHEL DE MONTAIGNE. Although these essays were written more than 400 years ago, Montaigne's musings on such subjects as education, parent-child relationships, friendship and various social customs are still remarkably astute. If there are educators in your book club, you will benefit greatly from the theories offered in this book.

FALLING OFF THE MAP: SOME LONELY PLACES OF THE WORLD, by PICO IYER. The inveterate Iyer travels to North Korea, Iceland, Buenos Aries and other spots to present the curious and the fantastical. If members of your group believe that the world is only as large as the local mall, this book is the perfect antidote.

THE FINANCIALLY INDEPENDENT WOMAN, by BARBARA LEE. Certainly any all-female book club will find it useful to discuss the different ways that women can thrive financially in today's world. This book, and other comprehensive guides like it, can offer long-term planning that club members can together use to assess their own future plans. A good read during income-tax season.

FROM BEIRUT TO JERUSALEM, by THOMAS L. FRIEDMAN. Everything you ever wanted to know about war and conflict in the Middle East but were too scared to ask. This work offers keen insight into the real issues behind the headlines and sound bites, with thorough and impartial clarity.

THE FUTURE OF THE RACE, by HENRY LOUIS GATES, JR., AND CORNELL WEST. Two brilliant thinkers take on the issue of race and its implications for the future of the black community in

America. Your group may want to read this alongside a work of fiction that addresses racism or prejudice.

THE HAPPY ISLES OF OCEANIA, by PAUL THEROUX. A remarkable account of paddling around the Pacific. Theroux is a traveller for whom the landscape puts "human effort into perspective." This book may very well lead your group to his other writings and worldly adventures.

A HISTORY OF READING, by ALBERTO MANGUEL. For all book lovers, readers and, of course, book clubs. Full of arcane information and curious intellectual pathways about all topics bookish, lovingly told.

HOTEL AMERICA, by LEWIS LAPHAM. A collection of essays by one of our century's most eloquent and iconoclastic thinkers. Your group may want to try a few essays at a time, rather than attempting to tackle the whole book at once.

HOW READING CHANGED MY LIFE, by ANNA QUINDLEN. A little book about reading for people who don't have time to read but still want to feel good about reading. Well, if you're in a book club already, this one's a nice pat on the back.

HOW THE IRISH SAVED CIVILIZATION, by THOMAS CAHILL. An illuminating book about the "island of saints and scholars." This engaging work of history will change the minds of any book club members who think that history is lifeless.

IN COLD BLOOD, by TRUMAN CAPOTE. Capote successfully melded fiction and journalism. He called this work, for example, a "non-fiction novel." It's the story of a multiple murder by two sociopaths, and your group will find it both riveting and horrific.

INDIA: A WOUNDED CIVILIZATION, by V. S. NAIPAUL. The great Trinidadian author of Indian descent goes to India to find himself disgusted by the corruption and filth. A complex study of personal discovery and identity, with which book club members will sympathize, regardless of their own ethnic origin.

THE INTERPRETATION OF DREAMS, by SIGMUND FREUD. If your book club is made up of ten men and their ten mothers, then this might just be the perfect book for you. No matter who is in your group, if you throw Freud on the table and share a few dreams you've had recently, all hell will break loose.

IN THE SPIRIT OF CRAZY HORSE, by PETER MATTHIESSEN. An eloquent naturalist, Matthiessen writes about the conflict between the American Indian Movement and federal agents at Wounded Knee, South Dakota, in 1963. Almost any Matthiessen book is worth your club's time and energy.

INTO THIN AIR, by JON KRAKAUER. A gripping account of the lengths people will go to achieve something they will always be able to brag about. Krakauer was part of an ill-fated expedition to the top of Everest in 1996, and he discusses his thoughts on how quickly climbers ignore better judgement when faced with all but insurmountable odds.

JAMES JOYCE, by RICHARD ELLMANN. It could be argued that the only thing as fascinating as Joyce's novels is his life. If you are reading any of Joyce's fiction, this biography is the perfect complement to your discussion. This 900-page monster may intimidate you, but you can start with the sections most relevant to your specific interests or your current reading.

JERUSALEM, by KAREN ARMSTRONG. The three religions that consider this city sacred are intent on destroying one another to have it. Your group will be mesmerized by the biblical and secular histories that brought us all to this point, and Armstrong, a former nun, is also a keen historian.

THE LAST GIFT OF TIME: LIFE BEYOND SIXTY, by CAROLYN HEILBRUN. Heilbrun also writes mysteries under the name Amanda Cross. Here she is a dispassionate observer of the effects that age and memory have on women. This is a tough book written by someone who remains intellectually and creatively engaged in all aspects of life.

THE LAST THREE MINUTES, by PAUL DAVIES. One of the most impassioned and eloquent of contemporary science writers, Davies speculates about the ultimate end of the universe. Your group may want to read Steven Weinberg's *The First Three Minutes* in tandem with this one.

LENIN'S TOMB: THE LAST DAYS OF THE SOVIET EMPIRE, by DAVID REMNICK. Now the editor of *The New Yorker*, Remnick was a reporter in the Soviet Union from 1988 to 1992. This book presents an enormous complex canvas of a culture in transition. Fortunately, the eloquent Remnick is up to the challenge.

LET US NOW PRAISE FAMOUS MEN, by JAMES AGEE AND WALKER EVANS. A classic, which tells in photographs and words the lives of tenant farmers in the Deep South of the 1930s. A poetic and unsentimental work that is unlike any other nonfiction your group will read.

LONG WALK TO FREEDOM, by NELSON MANDELA. A remarkable memoir by a person who has gone through more than most of us can ever imagine, including twenty-seven years in a South African prison. Your club will find it inspiring and ultimately uplifting.

LORD HIGH EXECUTIONER, by HOWARD ENGEL. One of
Canada's leading mystery writers, Engel takes his reader through
a relentless history of criminal executions. This book has some
truly bizarre moments, and will lead to some honest discussions
on the logic of capital punishment.

LOVING JESUS, by MOTHER THERESA. The modern-day saint
talks about the poor and the forgotten in society, as well as AIDS
and abortion. If your group is in a combative mood, try reading
this in tandem with *The Missionary Position*, by Christopher
Hitchens.

THE MAKING OF THE ATOMIC BOMB, by RICHARD RHODES.
Everything you ever wanted to know about the most powerful,
destructive discovery and invention we've ever known. Your book
group will be in awe at the speed of how quickly the Manhattan
Project moved from theory to devastating Hiroshima.

THE MALAISE OF MODERNITY, by CHARLES TAYLOR. A series of
essays that discuss the modern concept of self-fulfillment. A good
introduction for a group wanting to approach modern philosoph-
ical inquiry.

THE MAN WHO MISTOOK HIS WIFE FOR A HAT, by OLIVER
SACHS. Touching, tragic insights into the human condition told
by a distinguished and compassionate doctor. Your group will
marvel about the curious psychological paths the mind and body
can take.

MEN ARE FROM MARS, WOMEN ARE FROM VENUS, by JOHN
GRAY. Sure, we know this isn't the most sophisticated stuff, but if
your group is ever in the mood to read the book that everyone else
alive has read, and have that age-old argument about the differences between men and women, then why not give this one a spin?

MISOGYNIES, by JOAN SMITH. A classic and controversial collection of essays on the hatred of women. If your group is looking for a feisty work to get it out of the conversational doldrums, this might be just the ticket.

MY AMERICAN CENTURY, by STUDS TERKEL. This book collects fifty of Terkel's best conversations and interviews with ordinary people telling their own stories about war, their working life and their relationships. Terkel calls his books "oral journals" and this book is well worth a listen.

MY LIFE WITH THE CHIMPANZEES, by JANE GOODALL. Goodall is perhaps the most famous naturalist in the world today. Here she writes about her life-long fascination with and respect for African chimpanzees. It is a truly remarkable and inspiring autobiography.

A NARRATIVE OF THE CAPTIVITY AND RESTORATION OF MRS. MARY ROWLANDSON, by MARY ROWLANDSON. A seventeenth-century Puritan woman is taken prisoner by American natives and must survive by her wits. Hollywood could never do justice to the terror and heroism of this story. You may also want to discuss how much of the real story a Puritan woman can honestly relate after the fact.

NARRATIVE OF THE LIFE OF FREDERICK DOUGLASS, AN AMERICAN SLAVE, WRITTEN BY HIMSELF. It could be argued that the most reliable glimpse into the history of American slavery is through the eyes of a freed slave, and Douglass tells his story with clarity, intelligence and a profound understanding of the slave owner's psychology.

NIGHT, by ELIE WIESEL. No writer has painted a clearer and more terrifying depiction of life in a Nazi concentration camp than Wiesel does in his most famous book. This book should inspire some profound debates among book club members on the nature of evil and the spirit of survival.

ON ACTING, by LAURENCE OLIVIER. One of the world's most beloved actors takes you through a history of his outstanding career, with personal anecdotes and commentary on different acting styles. A witty autobiography best for theatre buffs, would-be actors and amateur film historians.

ON BOXING, by JOYCE CAROL OATES. An eloquent and sympathetic discourse on the sweet science, in all its brutishness and beauty. Although your group may think it shouldn't spend its time on a work about boxing, this brief book will change your mind.

ON LIES, SECRETS AND SILENCE, by ADRIENNE RICH. A feminist classic, important no matter what the gender mix is of your group, this book traces Rich's thoughts on "motherhood, racism, history, poetry, the uses of scholarship, the politics of language."

ON PHOTOGRAPHY, by SUSAN SONTAG. A series of brilliant essays on how photography has changed the way we see and understand the world. Your group may decide to read the whole book or just tackle one essay in a meeting.

ON THE TAKE, by STEVIE CAMERON. Corruption. Greed. Underhanded deals. The plot line of the newest Hollywood thriller? Not quite. Cameron's exposé of Canada's Mulroney era is still as relevant as it was when it first came out, warning us about the real dirt behind the scenes in any political forum.

ORIENTALISM, by EDWARD SAID. Said is one of the most important academic voices to have emerged out of the Arab world. This book, which explores the relationship between cultures, specifically how perceptions of the Muslim Orient have been constructed in the West, is for groups ready to tackle challenging, scholarly texts.

THE ORIGIN OF HUMANKIND, by RICHARD LEAKEY. The distinguished anthropologist unearths remarkable bones and fascinating observations. Your group will find much more to this book than mere documentation of excavating arid sites.

PALIMPSEST, by GORE VIDAL. Vidal has encountered more leaders of American culture and politics than almost any other American writer of the twentieth century. In this memoir, he shares his experiences, pointing out perceived contradictions with wit and almost frightening poignancy.

PILGRIM AT TINKER CREEK, by ANNIE DILLARD. A true original in the tradition of Henry David Thoreau, Dillard is known for her ability to bring together the visionary and the here-and-now. In these essays she is simultaneously meditative and concerned with the world at her doorstep.

THE POWER OF MYTH, by JOSEPH CAMPBELL. Campbell's primary strength was in looking back into ancient myths and finding their ongoing relevance in the contemporary world. His observations often inspire readers to look at their lives with new insight. This is a healthy exercise every once in a while, and group members will enjoy sharing their own relationships with shared myths.

PRAISE OF FOLLY, by ERASMUS. Feeling stupid? Wondering what motivated you to make that social faux pas at the office party last week? Let this great Renaissance scholar tell you why you should embrace that stupidity rather than fear it. This is a much funnier, lighter read than you would expect.

THE PRINCE, by NICCOLO DI MACHIAVELLI. This book should be subtitled "You've Got to Be Cruel to Be Kind." Machiavelli's name today is associated with all that is evil and underhanded in politics. But if your group returns to his most famous text, which is still amazingly readable, you may find it full of good, reasonable, sound advice.

THE RANTS, by DENNIS MILLER. This one will make you laugh until you start to feel very uneasy. Miller sees hypocrisy on the American right and left, and despite his comedic past and the great wit of this book, his insights on many of America's greatest recent social phenomena often cut close to the bone.

A ROOM OF ONE'S OWN, by VIRGINIA WOOLF. The title of this book has become a cliché in female and feminist art, but the ideas formulated by Woolf in this work about the personal and imaginative space necessary as conditions for women's creativity remain as important and vital today as they were during Woolf's lifetime.

RUNNING IN THE FAMILY, by MICHAEL ONDAATJE. A lyrical and often endearing biography of Ondaatje's early years in Ceylon. "A literary work is a communal act," says Ondaatje, which is an important concept for this book and your group.

SCORNED AND BELOVED: DEAD OF WINTER MEETINGS WITH CANADIAN ECCENTRICS, by BILL RICHARDSON. Not the most controversial book your book group will ever read, but there are some hilarious passages and some truly curious people discussed (including Richardson himself).

THE SECOND SEX, by SIMONE DE BEAUVOIR. A pioneering feminist text exploring different gender roles, the historical status of women in the world and the common threads between all women. This is the perfect starting point for any group that wants to explore feminist ideas and feminist novels.

SEXUAL PERSONAE, by CAMILLE PAGLIA. Paglia is the feminist's anti-feminist and vice versa. Her jarring insights on the relationship between the sexes will seem like heresy to some and just good common sense to others. This book will definitely spark some heated arguments in any crowd, particularly the mixed-gender book club.

SHADOW-MAKER: THE LIFE OF GWENDOLYN MACEWEN, by ROSEMARY SULLIVAN. An empathetic biography of the talented, vulnerable poet. For book clubs searching for contemporary literary biographies.

THE SKIN OF CULTURE: INVESTIGATING THE NEW ELECTRONIC REALITY, by DERRICK DE KERCKHOVE. For groups wanting to know what's around the next technological corner. The book is snappy, energetic and provocative, if sometimes a bit arcane.

A SLENDER THREAD, by DIANE ACKERMAN. A sensitive author tells of her work in a crisis centre while observing nature in her own backyard. Well worth the read, though some club members may find it a little precious.

A SOCIAL HISTORY OF MADNESS, by ROY PORTER. Focusing on historical figures, this book traces the ways that insane writers and thinkers offer a mirror image of the world around them. It will certainly get your group thinking about the madness of the world around them in new ways.

SOLITUDE: A RETURN TO THE SELF, by ANTHONY STORR. A challenging book on the uses of solitude and the important role of such experiences as despair and depression. It's not all doom, though. Storr also leads the reader through the search for meaning and the significance of interpersonal relationships.

THE SONGLINES, by BRUCE CHATWIN. A wise and colourful account of Chatwin's travels in the Australian Outback, where Aboriginals recount their history by singing songs of the land. It may inspire members of your group to head off to Patagonia or other exotic locales.

SPEAK, MEMORY, by VLADIMIR NABOKOV. Author of the notorious *Lolita*, Nabokov talks about his early years at his aristocratic family's estate in Russia and the Russian communities in Paris and Berlin. An excellent biographical introduction to all his writing.

STOLEN CONTINENTS, by RONALD WRIGHT. A well-intentioned writer lives among native tribes of the Americas in order to rewrite North American history from their point of view. Is this a sensitive look at a problematic history or just another white man pontificating and speaking for other groups?

THAT SUMMER IN PARIS, by MORLEY CALLAGHAN. This memoir could be subtitled "Punching Ernest Hemingway," after its best-known anecdote. Callaghan's reflections on his time among such legends as Hemingway and F. Scott Fitzgerald in the 1920s is a fitting tribute to the most famous group of expatriates this century.

THIS YEAR IN JERUSALEM, by MORDECAI RICHLER. The great Canadian satirist goes to Israel in search of his childhood Zionist friends who lived the dream and moved to Israel. Your group can address how this book quickly becomes a poignant study on the relationship between ideology and reality.

TIMESHIFTING, by STEPHAN RECHTSCHAFFEN. This book argues that one key to inner contentment is finding the time to do the things that allow you to develop personally and spiritually. One such exercise might be...joining a book club! This book may provide club members with some valuable hints on managing their time.

THE UNCONSCIOUS CIVILIZATION, by JOHN RALSTON SAUL. Feisty and passionate. This series of lectures argues that our society is increasingly conformist and corporatist. It will definitely get your club talking.

WALDEN, OR LIFE IN THE WOODS, by HENRY DAVID THOREAU. The ultimate treatise on simplifying life to discover the essential and the important. Okay, so Thoreau may have gone a little far in rejecting the materialism around him, but your group members will certainly have a good time confessing to their own excesses.

A WALK IN THE WOODS, by BILL BRYSON. Humourist Bryson tells the engaging tale of walking the 2,100 miles of the Appalachian Trail. Never one to take himself too seriously, Bryson manages to bring together a majestic landscape with his own clear-eyed insights.

WOODY ALLEN, by ERIC LAX. Whether you love him or hate him, there is no denying that Woody Allen has created one the most impressive bodies of work in American film history. Of course, this book was written before the whole Soon-Yi scandal, which should inspire some heated discussions.

THE WORST JOURNEY IN THE WORLD, by APSLEY CHERRY-GARRARD. A tragic and harrowing first-person account of Scott's last expedition to Antarctica. Your group may want to read this with one of the more pleasant or jovial travel books on this list, perhaps *A Year in Provence.*

A YEAR IN PROVENCE, by PETER MAYLE. For everyone who has dreamed of packing up and heading off to the south of France. A light read, full of stories of delicious eating, good humour and small town adventures. Why not encourage your group to read this while on a collective three-month holiday on the French Riviera?

THE YELLOW WIND, by DAVID GROSSMAN. Around the time that the Palestinian intifada was beginning, Grossman ventured into the West Bank to observe how Israeli settlers and Palestinians were interacting. His findings were shocking, and many Israeli groups attempted to ban this angry, terrifying book.

And One More for Good Measure

BUILD A BETTER BOOK CLUB, by HARRY HEFT AND PETER O'BRIEN. Witty, charming, wise, sparkling, articulate, vital, entertaining, touching, clever, helpful, thought-provoking, book club-provoking, sensible, snappy. The only weakness in this book is that the authors are too modest. A must read!

HARRY HEFT is the co-author of the Macmillan Canada book, *On Your Mark: Getting Better Grades Without Working Harder or Being Smarter*, which is being published in the United States as *The Savvy Student* by Avon Books. He has written book reviews and articles for *The Financial Post*, *The Mystery Review*, and numerous other publications. He has also taught English Literature, Creative Writing and Cinema at the University of Western Ontario, King's College, and the Hebrew University of Jerusalem. Although his book club has complained that he speaks too loudly and too often, they have thus far not asked him to leave.

PETER O'BRIEN is the editor of *So to Speak: Interviews with Contemporary Canadian Writers* (Vehicule); and the co-editor of *Introduction to Literature: British, American, Canadian* (Harper & Row) and *Fatal Recurrences: New Fiction in English from Montreal* (Vehicule). He was the founding editor of Rubicon, a literary and art journal; was co-editor of *Descant* literary magazine; and is currently a contributing editor of *DA: A Journal of the Printing Arts*. His reviews and articles have appeared in many publications, including *The Globe and Mail*, *The Montreal Gazette*, *The Toronto Star*, *National Post*, *Canadian Art* and *Books in Canada*. He has been a member of book clubs in several cities and with various groupings of people.

PAUL QUARRINGTON is a novelist and playwright. His books include *Whale Music*, for which he won the 1991 Governor General's Award, *The Boy on the Back of the Turtle* and most recently, *The Spirit Cabinet*. In 1987 he received the Stephen Leacock Award for Humour, and in 1991 he was awarded a Genie for his screenplay "Perfectly Normal". He lives in Toronto, in case you want to invite him to a book club meeting.